The Equine Legal Handbook

Gary R. Katz

Half Halt Press
Middletown, Maryland

The Equine Legal Handbook

Published 1993 in the United States of America by

Half Halt Press, Inc.
6416 Burkittsville Road
Middletown, MD 21769

Book and cover design by Clara Graves

Printed in the United States of America

Table of Contents

Foreword

This book is dedicated to all the hard working horsemen in the world who have been living in the twentieth century while doing business in the same fashion as their nineteenth century predecessors. The fact is that the horse industry has managed to do business far too long with the simple handshake being the customary practice for making agreements. As a result, too many business transactions in the horse industry today still occur without the benefit of the any written contract between the parties, or without any type of writing specifying the basic understanding of an agreement between parties. Consequently, when problems later arise, it is too late for the conscientious horseman to be protected. In order to correct this problem, I have attempted to create simple contracts for the everyday use by horsemen. Use of a written contract makes only sound business sense. Proper use of the contracts presented here can only enhance the way a professional or non-professional does "business" and will, virtually guaranteed, save those individuals substantial time as well money toward legal costs at some point in the future. Of course, there can be no guarantee that the use of these contracts will prevent future litigation, but the proper and judicious use of these contracts can and will help protect your business and your assets to the maximum extent possible under the present day laws.

It should be noted that these contracts are sample forms only, and should be tailored for each horseman's particular needs. Although the particular contract form presented may be sufficient in many cases, it is highly recommended that an interested party have competent legal counsel review any contract prior to his or execution of the agreement. The forms presented in this book should give any horseman, or his attorney, the basis for preparing any of the types of contracts listed herein.

I sincerely hope that horsemen will find these contracts useful in their daily activities with horses and that they will, in fact, use them to their benefit and protection, as part of their business or pleasure activity, whichever the case may be. The world has changed substantially from the nineteenth century to the present day-it is essential that today's horseman change with it.

Gary R. Katz

Boarding Agreements

A "contract" has been defined as where one party promises to perform a service in return for another party's promise to tender payment for the performance of same. It can be further defined as being an agreement between two or more persons to do or not to do a particular thing; and the "obligation" of a contract is found in the terms in which the contract is expressed and is the duty thus assumed by the contracting parties respectively to perform the stipulation of such contract. A writing which contains the agreement of the parties, with the terms and conditions, serves as proof of the obligation.

An express contract is an actual agreement of the parties, the terms of which are openly uttered or declared at the time of the making it, being stated in distinct and explicit language, either orally or in writing. An implied contract is one not created or evidenced by the explicit agreement of the parties, but inferred by the law, as a matter of reason and justice from their acts or conduct, the circumstances surrounding the transaction making it a reasonable, or even necessary, assumption that a contract existed between them by tacit understanding.

Anytime a horse owned by Party A is being boarded or otherwise being taken care by Party B, an express boarding agreement between the panics, as described above, becomes essential. Although that express agreement can be oral or in writing, certainly there are distinct advantages to putting the express agreement in writing. The written agreement should outline each party's responsibilities with regard to the care and maintenance of the horse in question. Any basic understanding between the parties should be spelled out as specifically as possible, in order to eliminate, as much as possible, the potential for misunderstanding in the future and the subsequent need for third parties (i.e. the courts) to interpret and otherwise enforce the contract on the basis of what each party thought or otherwise believed to be their understanding of the agreement. Consequently, the more specific the terms of the contract, the less room for misunderstanding in the future.

In a boarding agreement, the owner of the horse is mostly interested in making sure his or her horse will be well taken care of, while the "Farm" is most interested in providing a service and getting paid for same. With regard to any agreement, "consideration" is necessary to have a valid contract. "Consideration" is the payment or inducement to the Farm in return for providing the services. Therefore, the consideration in the boarding agreement is the monthly board paid for the horse by the Owner. Failure to make these payments when required can result in the Farm's right to a lien against the horse and can ultimately lead either directly or indirectly to a subsequent sheriff's sale of the horse for the amount owed for the board.

Because of liability, insurance has become increasingly an issue and, thus, should also be addressed in the boarding agreement itself. If the Owner of a horse is expected or required to have coverage of any kind (e.g. liability insurance), it should be specifically stated in the agreement. "Hold Harmless" clauses are also often needed in the basic boarding agreement to protect the parties and should be a requirement in today's litigious environment. All parties should fully understand the repercussions of any release, waiver, and/or hold harmless agreement in order that an intelligent and voluntary decision can be made regarding such a release or waiver of liability.

The first boarding agreement in this section would generally be used by independent contractors in more of a farm situation, for example, for lay ups. The second agreement would be used for a commercial establishment, a riding stable, for example. However, the phraseology with regard to terms and conditions in the agreements is interchangeable to meet the needs of the particular situation.

In addition, a list of fees charged for extra services should be included as an addendum to the agreement. These might include such things as charges for administering required medications, changing blankets, grooming, and so on.

Boarding Agreement #1

THIS AGREEMENT, dated this day of ____________, 19____ is made between ____________________________________ hereinafter referred to as "FARM", an independent contractor, located at ____ and _______________ ______________________ residing at __________________________ ______________________, owner of the below described horse(s), hereinafter referred to as "OWNER".

A. FEES AND TERM: LOCATION

In consideration of $__________ per horse per month paid by OWNER in advance on the _________ day of each month, FARM agrees to board the herein described horses at ________________________ commencing on a month to month basis.

B. DESCRIPTION OF HORSE(S)

NAME:_______________________________________

AGE:____

COLOR:______________________________________

SEX:____

BREED:______________________________________

REGISTRATION/TATTOO NO:____________________
(If applicable)

C. FEED AND FACILITIES:

FARM agrees to provide the following, in addition to normal and reasonable care required to maintain the health and well-being of the animal:

_____________________ stall
(Minimum size)

_____________________ pasture or paddock (turn-out) on a daily basis
(Maximum # horses)

_______________________ grain (specify type, if applicable) per
(Pounds)
day fed ______ times per day.

_______________________ hay (specify type, if applicable) per
(Pounds)
day fed ______ times per day.

D. EXERCISE: FARM (will will/not) provide exercise or any other care for said horse(s).

E. SPECIAL INSTRUCTIONS TO FARM:

[List: any special instruction to the farm with regard to the care of the horse.]

F. RIGHT OF LIEN: The OWNER is put on notice that FARM has a right of lien, as set forth in the law of the State of_________________________ for the amount due for the board and keep of such horse (s) and shall have the right without process of law, to retain said horse(s) until the amount of indebtedness is discharged.

G. RISK OF LOSS-INSURANCE: It is agreed that during the term of this agreement the risk of said horse(s) shall be assumed by OWNER, and in the event of loss or injury of the horses and OWNER agrees to hold FARM harmless from any loss or injury to said horse(s).

H. EMERGENCY CARE: FARM agrees to attempt to contact OWNER should FARM feel that medical treatment is needed for said

horses but if FARM is unable to contact OWNER within a reasonable time, FARM is then authorized to secure emergency veterinary and/or blacksmith care required for the health and well-being of said horse(s). The cost of such care secured shall be paid by OWNER within fifteen days from the day OWNER receives notice thereof or FARM is authorized as OWNER'S agent to arrange direct billing to the OWNER.

I. HOLD HARMLESS: OWNER agrees to hold FARM harmless from any damages caused to FARM property by OWNER or his horse(s), and from any claim resulting from damage or an injury caused by said horse(s) except when caused by negligence of FARM.

Optional Clause:
[OWNER agrees to carry liability insurance protecting OWNER and FARM from any such claim in the following amounts: $____________ personal injury, $_______________ maximum per accident; $______________ property damage; $_____________ maximum per accident.

If said insurance is required, OWNER shall provide FARM with certificates of said insurance prior to acceptance of said animal for boarding by FARM, naming FARM additional insured.]

J. OWNERSHIP: OWNER warrants that he owns said horse (s) and that there are no liens against said horse (s), express or implied by law.

K. DEFAULT: Either party may terminate this Agreement for failure of the other party to meet any material terms of this

Agreement. In the case of any default by one party, the other party shall have the right to recover attorney's fees and court costs as a result of said default.

L. TERMINATION: This lease is at month to month tenancy and either party may, terminate this lease by giving the other party thirty days written notice thereof.

IT IS UNDERSTOOD by the parties that pursuant to state law, the FARM has a lien on said horse(s) to secure payment for services to be provided by FARM hereunder, and that if OWNER should not pay same that FARM may sell said horse (s) at private or public auction pursuant to state law.

THIS AGREEMENT is subject to the laws of the State of ______________________.

EXECUTED at ____________________________ this __________ day of ______________, 19____.

OWNER	**FARM**
______________________ (Name)	______________________ (Manager)
______________________ (Address)	______________________ (Address)
______________________	______________________
______________________ (Phone Number)	______________________ (Phone Number)

Boarding Agreement #2

THIS AGREEMENT, dated the ________________ day of ______________, 19____ made between ________________________________ a corporation of the State of ____________________ with its principal office located at ____ ____________________ hereinafter called "STABLE"; and __________ ____________________ residing at ______________________________ ______________________________ hereinafter called "OWNER".

1. FEES, TERM & LOCATION.

In consideration of $____________________ per horse per month paid by OWNER in advance on the _____________ day of each month, STABLE agrees to board the herein described horse(s) at STABLE located at ____ commencing on ____________________ for a period of ______________ months.

2. DESCRIPTION OF HORSE(S).

1) Name ________________________________
2) Age __________________________________
3) Color ________________________________
4) Breed ________________________________
5) Sex __________________________________
6) Registration # _____________________
(if applicable)

3. FEED & FACILITIES. STABLE agrees to provide adequate feed and facilities for normal and reasonable care required to maintain the health and well being of the animal. STABLE will provide a minimum stall size for one horse, ___________________ in size.

4. EXERCISE. The OWNER shall be solely responsible for the exercise of the animal(s) and it is expressly understood by the OWNER that the horse(s) (will/will not) be turned out.

5. RISK OF LOSS. During the time that the horse is in custody of STABLE, STABLE shall not be liable for any sickness, disease, theft, death or injury which may be suffered by the horse or any other cause of action, whatsoever, arising out of or being connected in any way with the boarding of said horse(s). This includes, but is not limited to, any personal injury or disability the horse may receive while on STABLE'S premises. The OWNER fully understands that STABLE does not carry any insurance on any horses not owned by it for boarding or for any other purposes, for which the horse(s) are covered under any public liability, accidental injury, theft or equine mortality insurance and that all risks connected with boarding or for any other reason for which the horse is in the possession on the premises of STABLE, are to be borne by the OWNER.

6. HOLD HARMLESS. OWNER agrees to hold STABLE harmless from any claim resulting from damage or injury caused by said horse to anyone and agrees to pay any legal fees, and/or expenses incurred by STABLE in defense of such claims.

7. EMERGENCY CARE. STABLE agrees to attempt to contact OWNER should STABLE feel that medical treatment is needed for said horse(s) but, if STABLE is unable to contact OWNER, STABLE is then authorized to secure emergency veterinary and/or blacksmith care required for the health and well being of said horse(s). All costs of such care secured shall be paid by OWNER

within fifteen days from the date OWNER receives notice thereof, or STABLE is authorized, as OWNER'S agent, to arrange direct billing to the OWNER.

8. **SHOEING & WORMING.** STABLE agrees to provide the necessary shoeing and worming of the horse as is reasonably necessary. However, such expense for the same shall be the obligation of the OWNER, upon presentation by STABLE of the bill for such services rendered, including service charges, such bill shall be paid within fifteen days from the date the bill is submitted to the OWNER.

9. **GROOMING.** STABLE (shall/shall not) provide reasonable grooming for said horse(s) and (shall/shall not) become part of and included within the aforesaid fees.

10. **OWNERSHIP—COGGINS TEST.** OWNER warrants that he owns said horse(s) and will provide, prior to the time of delivery of said animal(s), to STABLE, proof satisfactory to STABLE of a negative Coggins test.

11. **DEFAULT.** Either party may terminate this Agreement for failure of the other party to meet any material terms of this agreement. In the case of any default by one party, the other party shall have the right to recover attorney's fees and court costs incurred as a result of said default.

12. **ASSIGNMENT.** This Agreement cannot be assigned by the OWNER without the express written consent of STABLE.

13. NOTICE OF TERMINATION. OWNER agrees that thirty (30) days notice shall be given to STABLE as to the termination of this agreement.

14. RIGHT OF LIEN. The OWNER is put on notice that STABLE has a right of lien, as set forth in the law of the State of __________________. for the amount due for the board and keep of such horse(s) , and also for such storage and shall have the right, without process of law, to retain the said horse(s) until the amount of such indebtedness is discharged.

THIS AGREEMENT IS SUBJECT to the laws of the State of ____________________.

Executed at _________________________ this _____________ day of _________________, 19_____.

"STABLE"	"OWNER"
______________________	______________________
By	
______________________	______________________
Address	Address
______________________	______________________
______________________	______________________
Telephone	Telephone

Breeding Contracts

Breeding contracts can be fairly simple or more complex depending on the services to be rendered by the Stud Farm. Again, the more terms and conditions specifically described in the agreement, the less chance for a later misunderstanding between the parties. And, if problems do arise in the future, and legal action needs to be taken by one party or the other, the fact that there is a written agreement, with the terms and conditions specified, will provide protection to the party needing it.

Normally, the breeding contract is executed by the parties prior to the delivery of the mare to the Stud Farm. Usually, a stud farm will require various health certificates and negative Coggins test before the mare can be accepted for breeding purposes.

Another point of note regarding breeding contracts is the various definitions of "live foal" guarantees as it relates to refunds or future breedings. Is the "live foal" defined as getting up and nursing or is it defined as being alive for a specified period of time? Under the guarantee, if there is one, does the Owner of the mare get a re-breeding to the same stallion at no additional charge the next breeding season or does he/she get a credit or refund for all or pan of the breeding fee and costs for the season in which the mare was bred?

As with the boarding contracts, there may be liability insurance requirements while the mare is being boarded and maintained at the stud farm. Mortality insurance is also a consideration for both mare and foal under the breeding contract and should be addressed by the parties. It should be noted that no matter how careful farm management may be, horses can and do get hurt, or get sick, and there is little that a farm can do to prevent it. Normally, the farm can limit its liability for any injury or death of a horse if the farm has acted in the way of the "ordinary prudent and reasonable man." However, even with release of liability and hold harmless language in a contract, the farm can and probably will be held liable if it has acted in a grossly negligent or reckless nature and not in a customary and prudent manner that is the standard normally demanded by the law.

Also enclosed in the following documents is the Information Form for Mares which normally accompanies the Booking or Breeding Agreement. This document is for informational purposes only and is recommended to be included as part of any booking/breeding agreement so as to provide a complete medical background of the mare if the stud farm does not already have one.

Breeding Contract #1

THIS AGREEMENT is made this ______________ day of ____________, 19____, by and between ____________________________ (Owner of Stallion) hereinafter referred to as ______________________, (Farm) and ______________________________ (Owner of Mare) hereinafter referred to as ____________________ (Owner).

A. Inconsideration of $____________ (Stud Fee), ____________________ (Owner of Stallion) ____________ hereby agrees to breed his stallion ____________ ______________________ (Name, Description, Tattoo Number) to ______________________ (Owner of Mare)'s mare, __________________________ (Name, Description, Tattoo Number).

B. __________________________________ (Owner of Mare) agrees to pay said $______________ (Stud Fee) on the dates indicated below:

Date	Amount
______________________	______________________
______________________	______________________

C. In the event that ________________________ (Owner of Mare)'s mare does not take and become in foal, ________________________ (Owner of Stallion) agrees to breed said mare again for $____________________ (Additional Fee) additional consideration at any time prior to __________________ (Date).

In the event said mare does not deliver a live foal, ____________________________ (Owner of Stallion) agrees to give ___________ (Owner of Mare) ______________________ the right to an additional service to said mare (at any time within ____________________ (Term of Time)) from the last date of breeding said mare under this contract.

____________________________ shall have no further liability
(Owner of Stallion)
hereunder for servicing said mare. For the purposes of this Agreement, "Live Foal" means "standing and nursing."

D. ________________________________ warrants that said mare
(Owner of Mare)
is free from disease or infection that could be transmitted to said stallion, and agrees to provide and pay for a veterinarian certificate, showing such freedom of disease or infection.

E. In addition to the above charge for breeding ______________
(Owner of Mare)
__________________ agrees to pay the following:

1. $______________ a day for feed and board;
(Rates)

2. $______________ a day for exercise of said mare as described
(Rates)
below.

F. __________________________________ agrees to provide the
(Owner of Stallion)
following for the fees indicated:

1. Feed: (Describe)

______________ of hay per feeding;
(Pounds)

______________ of grain per feeding;
(Pounds)

______________ of feedings per day.
(Number)

2. Stall: (Describe)

3. Turn-out/Pasture: (Describe)

4. Exercise: (Describe)

G. ___________________________ agrees to assume the risk of
(Owner of Mare)
injury, sickness or death to said mare except where caused by negligence of _____________________________, his agent's officer or employee.
(Owner of Stallion)

H. ______________________________ agrees to indemnify and hold
(Owner of Mare)
____________________________ harmless for any loss or injury due
(Owner of Stallion)
to acts of said mare while on premises or under control of ____________________________ except where caused by negligence
(Owner of Stallion)
of____________________________.
(Owner of Stallion)

To protect against said loss or injury, _______________________
(Owner of Mare)
__________________ agrees to secure liability insurance in the amount of $__________________ for personal injury per accident, and $__________________ per injury, and $_________________ property damage and to provide a certificate of insurance having named additional insured. (*1)

I. If prior to the breeding of said mare or after the mare has been bred but not come in foal, said stallion or mare dies or becomes unfit for service as so declared by a licensed veterinarian, then this Agreement shall become null and void and all monies paid by ________________________________, not
(Owner of Mare)
including expenses, shall be refunded.

(Or, mare owner shall have no right to a refund hereunder, but shall have the option of using the following stallions of the owner at the charges indicated [or indicated refund will be given])

____
(Alternative Stallion)

____
(Alternative Stallion)

J. ________________________________ agrees to use reasonable
(Owner of Stallion)
care and caution for said mare while in his possession or

control, pursuant to this Agreement and is authorized to obtain any necessary veterinarian or horseshoing care as required, but only after taking steps to contact ________________________ (Owner of Mare) ______________ without success.

K. As used herein, "Live Foal" means:

(Define e.g., "Standing and Nursing"; "Breathing", etc.)

L. ________________________ (Owner of Stallion) agrees to execute all necessary documents of the registration of the offspring of the breeding and should he fail or be unable to do so, ________________________ (Owner of Mare) is hereby authorized to so execute on behalf of ________________________ (Owner of Stallion) as his agent. (*2)

M. This Agreement is governed and shall be construed under the laws of the State of ________________________.

N. Either party may terminate this Agreement for failure of other party to meet any material terms of this Agreement. In the case of any default by one party, the other party shall have the right to recover attorney's fees and court costs incurred as a result of said default.

________________________	________________________
(Owner of Stallion)	(Owner of Mare)
________________________	________________________
(Address)	(Address)
________________________	________________________

*1 This clause is optional.

*2 Note: The involved Registry may or may not accept this agency appointment and a stallion owner may be reluctant to appoint the owner of the mare as agent, depending on who the owner of the mare is.

Breeding Contract #2

THIS AGREEMENT, made and entered into this _____________ day of _____________, 19____, by and between _______________ _______________ residing at _______________ _______________, hereinafter referred to as "Mare Owner" and _______________, located at _______________, hereinafter referred to as "Stud Farm".

WITNESSETH,

WHEREAS, Farm is the owner of _______________ (Owner of Stallion) a _______________ (Age) year old, _______________ (Color), _______________ (Breed), tattoo # _______________ (If Applicable), and the Mare Owner is the owner of the mare named _______________ (Name of Mare) tattoo # _______________ (If Applicable), described as a _______________ (Color) _______________ mare, foaled in 19____, by _______________ (Sire) Reg. No. _______________ (If applicable) and, out of _______________ (Dam) _______________, due to foal _______________ (If Applicable).

AND WHEREAS, _______________ (Name of Stallion) will stand at stud during the 19____ season at Stud Farm, and the parties hereto desire to contract for the services of the Mare Owner one season's booking for 19____ to _______________ (Name of Stallion) for the services of the mare.

NOW THEREFORE, it is agreed as follows:

1. Upon payment of $_______________ (Amount) booking fee, which is not refundable, Stud Farm does hereby reserve for the Mare-Owner

one season's booking for 19____ to ______________________________
(Name of Stallion)
for the services of the mare.

2. (a) The mare shall remain at the Stud Farm for a sufficient time to be pregnancy-checked after having been bred.

(b) Board at the rate of $____________________ per day for
(Amount)
the keeping and ordinary care of the mare and/or foal will be paid by the Mare Owner.

(c) The balance of the Breeding Fee, $____________________
(Amount)
plus all unpaid board and expenses, will be paid when the mare is picked up.

3. Upon arrival, all mares shall be accompanied by a health certificate indicating current vaccination for equine influenza (strangles, tetanus, and sleeping sickness are also recommended) . Mares not accompanied by such certificate will be vaccinated shortly after arrival at expense of Mare Owner.

4. The Mare Owner agrees to allow Stud Farm to have a qualified veterinarian check the mare for normal breeding conditions, and to perform such other veterinary services that Stud Farm may deem necessary for the proper treatment and protection of the mare and/or foal at side. This is to be at the Mare Owner's expense and will be billed and paid prior to the mare is picked up.

5. During the time that the mare is in the custody of Stud Farm, Stud Farm shall not be liable for any sickness, disease, theft, death or injury which may be suffered by the mare and/or foal at her side or any other cause of action whatsoever arising out of or being connected in any way with breeding or boarding of the mare and/or foal. This includes, but is not limited to, any personal injury or disability which the Mare Owner may receive while on Stud Farm premises. The Mare Owner

fully understands that Stud Farm does not carry any outside insurance on horse(s) that are in their possession for breeding and boarding any public liability, accidental injury, theft or equine morality insurance policy and that all risks connected with breeding and boarding of the mare or mares are to be born by the Mare Owner.

6. Stud Farm guarantees a return breeding the following season provided the stallion is able to service mares either for said mare or an approved substitute should a live foal not result from this mating. For the purposes of this Agreement, a live foal shall be one that stands and nurses without assistance. This is to be evidenced by a written statement from a qualified veterinarian within one (1) week from death. In the event the stallion is not able to re-service said mare, Stud Farm may substitute another stallion at Mare Owner's option or all monies paid by Mare owner for the previous service, not including expenses, shall be refunded to Mare Owner.

7. Mares that are not halter broken or cannot be hobbled will not be accepted.

8. Stud Farm requires a negative Coggins Test for Equine Infectious Anemia (Swamp Fever) prior to mare's arrival at Stud Farm.

9. This contract shall not be assigned or transferred by either party hereto without the consent of the other. If the mare is to be rebred and the Mare Owner fails to deliver her for breeding the following year, then any and all fees paid shall not be refundable and this contract is thereby cancelled.

Stud Farm

Mare Owner	Manager

Breeding Booking Contract

____
(Farm Name)

____
(Street Address)

____
(City, State, Zip Code)

BOOKING CONTRACT, SEASON OF ______________
(Year)

Owner of Mare ______________________ Telephone No. ____________

Street Address/Route ____________________ City ____________

State ______________ Zip Code ______________

Name of Mare __________________________ Color ____________

Year Foaled ______________ Tattoo No. ________________

Sire: ______________________ Dam: ____________________

By: ____________________ In Foal To: ____________________

Date Due To Foal In: __________ To Be Bred To: ______________

Service Fee: ________________

(a) The mare is booked specifically by name and the booking may not be transferred to another mare without the prior written consent of Farm.

(b) Farm, its agents, employees, and the owners of the Stallion shall not be liable for injury, death or disability suffered by any animal from any cause whatsoever, while in its custody and the owner specifically asserts to such condition and waives

each and every claim for damages resulting from any such injury, death or disability.

(c) The service fee is due and payable when the mare has a live foal or ownership thereof changes, whichever comes first. A 1 % service charge will be added to any balance over 30 days. A live foal is one that is able to stand up and suckle. If the mare fails to produce a live foal, a service fee paid in advance shall be refunded upon receipt of a certificate from a veterinarian stating specifically that the mare has been pronounced barren after leaving Farm or has slipped her foal or has given birth to a dead foal, in which event the certificate must be presented to Farm no later than thirty (30) days after foaling. In the event of a slipped foal, a service fee will be refunded only if the mare had at least two vaccinations during pregnancy for Equine Rhinopneurmitis (Contagious abortion). Unless such vaccinations were given by Farm, a veterinarian's statement giving the date of such vaccinations must accompany the claim for a refund. In the event that the mare is sold, the service fee, if unpaid, shall immediately become due and payable and no refund shall be due from Farm unless such refund is guaranteed by it in writing prior to her sale.

(d) In the event the Stallion shall die, be removed from the Farm, or in any way become unfit for service prior to serving the mare, or if the mare should die or otherwise become unfit to be bred, then this contract is and shall be null and void.

(e) Farm reserves the right to reject any mare not in good condition or one that is vicious or unmanageable or not

standard and registered by ______________________ (Breed Registry).

No barren mare or one who has foaled under suspicious circumstances will be bred until she is cultured and found free of any genital tract infectious. After said tests are made, the necessary time for completion will have to be allowed. No blind mares are accepted without previous written authority of the Farm.

(f) The mare must have proof of a negative Coggins test for Equine Infectious Anemia (Swamp Fever). A certificate that the mare was tested within 30 days prior to her arrival at the Farm must accompany the mare. Each mare sent to Farm must have an identification tag on the halter.

(g) The opening and closing dates of the Farm breeding season are determined solely by the Farm.

Date of Contract: ______________________

Farm ______________________

Owner ______________________ By: ______________________ Manager

Information Form for Mares

(To be attached to Booking Contract)

BEING BOOKED TO

______________________________ FARM STALLIONS

Owner's Name ________________________ Phone No. ______________

Address ____

(Street) (City) (State)

____

(Mare's Name/Tattoo No.)

____

(Sire's Sire)

____

(Sire)

____

(Sire's Dam)

____

(Mare)

____

(Dam's Sire)

____

(Dam)

____

(Dam's Dam)

Age ____________________ Color ______________________

Markings ____

Anticipated arrival date ______________________________

Foal at side ______________ Sire of Foal_______________

Date of last foaling __________________________________

Is mare to remain at breeding farm until pregnancy check? _____

Does Mare have any dangerous propensities? If yes, describe below.

Medical History of mare:

Colic _______________ Frequency _____________________

Founder ______________ When __________________________

Allergies, if known ___________________________________

Other ____

Tetanus Toxois _____________________ Date _____________

VEE ____

Enciphalomyelitis (sleeping sickness),

Eastern & Western strains _____________________________

Date of last worming __________________________________

Breeding History:

Date of last breeding _________________________________

Problems, if any ______________________________________

Medications ____

____

Hormones (F.S.H., L.H., Progesterone), if used: ______________

Other____

Feeding Program:

Hay type ____________________ Amount ______________________

Grain type/s ________________ Amount ______________________

Pellets _____________________ Amount ______________________

Known Allergies to feeds __________________________________

Special Care Requirement __________________________________

____

____

Habits ____

____

____

To be contacted in case of emergency, if owner cannot be reached: ____

Name Phone Number

____

Address

Is mare insured?_____________________

By whom:

____

Name of Insurance Company Phone Number

____

Address

____

Amount of Insurance

____

Name of Insurance Agency (If applicable)

Breeding Agreement/Foal Exchange

This type of agreement or contract is desirable when an owner of a mare cannot afford the breeding or booking fee to a particular stallion to which he wishes to breed. Very often, a breeding farm may still agree to the breeding of the mare on the basis of several different types of mutually agreed upon arrangements.

One arrangement is where the Farm and Owner alternate ownership of the resulting foals on a biannual basis, with the owner of the mare being responsible for paying only the boarding cost for the mare. For example, the first foal might be designated to be for the Farm's exclusive ownership and use, and the second or subsequent foal might be designated for the Owner's exclusive possession, ownership and use, or vice versa. This type of arrangement can continue for a term agreed upon and stated in the agreement or may continue for an indefinite period of time as mutually agreed to by the parties.

Another arrangement is for the Farm and Owner to share ownership of the foal resulting from the breeding, intending for the foal to be sold at an appropriate time and the profit from the sale distributed on a predetermined, mutually agreed upon basis, which is very often, but not always, a simple 50/50 split.

In any case, such breeding arrangements have been made popular where the financial constraints of breeding a certain mare to a certain stallion are significant and where the stud farm would, otherwise, be very interested in a breeding between its stallion and the subject mare.

Breeding Contract
(Foal Exchange)

THIS AGREEMENT is entered into this ________________ day of ____________, 19____ by and between __________________________, residing at ____ hereinafter referred to as "Owner", and __________________________ (Farm Name) ____________, located at ____________________________________ ____ hereinafter referred to as "Farm."

Whereas, Owner owns a ________ year-old _______________ mare named ____, Registration #_______________________, foaled _______________, and,

Whereas, the parties hereto desire to breed said mare to said stallion and to each receive a foal therefrom, and to agree on the terms and conditions thereof.

NOW, THEREFORE, it is hereby agreed as follows:

1. Farm agrees to breed said owner's mare to Farm's stallion, ______________________________ (Name of Stallion), in the 19____ breeding season, prior to _______________________ (Date) and upon declaration in foal by a duly licensed veterinarian to advise owner thereof.

2. Owner agrees to deliver said mare to Farm for breeding in 19____ and upon being advised that the mare is in foal, pursuant to Paragraph 1 above, to secure said mare from Farm and to thereafter maintain her.

3. Should Owner fail to secure said mare from Farm after notice, then owner shall pay Farm $_____________ per day for the care, feed and boarding by Farm.

4. Owner agrees to pay, all veterinarian and farrier care required during the term of this Agreement for said mare.

5. Farm agrees to provide reasonable breeding conditions and facilities, furnish proper feed, water, shelter and exercise at Farm's expense, and to obtain veterinary and farrier care as required at owner's expense. All shall be provided in a manner consistent with good horse breeding practices in the State of ______________________________.

6. Upon foaling, or when earlier directed by Farm, the mare and foal shall be returned for breeding to Farm. The mare may be returned to Owner when pronounced in foal or at such time as directed by Farm, but no later than when the foal has been weaned. Farm shall inform Owner as to when to secure said mare and thereafter owner shall pay Farm $ __________ per day for feed, care and boarding by Farm.

7. Should Farm's stallion, ________________________________, (Name of Stallion) not place the mare in foal during the 19____ breeding season, Farm at its option may terminate this Agreement or substitute another stallion of their choice. Should said mare not be available for reasons beyond control of Owner, Farm may terminate this Agreement or select another mare of Owner for use herein.

8. Should the mare not produce a live foal then owner may terminate this Agreement or continue on the same terms and conditions as set forth herein including these paragraphs 7 and 8, until a live foal is received.

9. "Live Foal" as used in this Agreement shall mean the foal has stood and nursed from a mare or has been fed by hand, in each case for a period of at least 24 hours from the time of birth.

10. After Farm has received its foal pursuant to the terms of this Agreement, should for any reason Farm's stallion not bring said mare in foal or be unavailable for breeding for reasons beyond control of Farm, Owner, at his option, may request any other stallion owned by Farm be used for breeding of said mare.

11. After Farm has received its foal pursuant to the terms hereunder and should said mare not be available for whatever reason, Owner may use any other mare provided Farm consents thereto. Farm shall promptly advise Owner of its decision on any such substitute mare.

12. All veterinarian fees or charges related to the foal of Farm (i.e., the first foal) shall be assumed by Farm from the time of birth. Birth is defined as the time the foal has completely left the body of the mare and the umbilical cord has been broken. Veterinarian care related to the foaling of the mare shall be deemed mare veterinarian expenses and assumed by Owner.

13. All veterinarian fees and charges related to the foal of owner (i.e. the second foal) shall be assumed by Owner.

14. Title and risk of loss shall pass to Farm 24 hours after the moment of birth of its foal.

15. Farm has no duty to insure said mare during the term hereof. Both parties during the term hereof shall maintain a liability insurance policy with reasonable limits to cover the liability for injury to persons or damage to property caused by said mare or stallion.

16. Owner agrees not to lease or sell said mare without expressly providing in a sale or lease agreement terms to

protect the rights of Farm hereunder and without obtaining Farm's written approval of said sale or lease.

17. Owner agrees to provide reasonable care and maintenance of Farm's foal while in his care at no cost.

18. If either party hereto shall default with respect to any material condition or covenant hereof, by him to be performed, the other party may, but need not, declare this Agreement to be terminated. The breaching party shall be responsible to the other party for reasonable attorney's fees and court costs related to any breach.

19. No delay or omission to exercise any right, power, or remedy accruing to either party on any breach or default of this Agreement shall impair any such right, power, or remedy of said party, nor shall it be construed to be a waiver of any such breach or default, or an acquiescence therein, or in any similar breach or default thereafter or thereafter occurring. Any waiver, permit, or approval of any kind or character on the part of either party of any breach or default under this Agreement, or any waiver on the part of the other party of any provision of condition of this Agreement must be in writing and should be effective only to the extent in such writing specifically set forth. All remedies, either under this Agreement or by law, or otherwise afforded to either party shall be cumulative and not alternative.

20. The provisions of this lease shall be binding on the heirs, executors, administrators and assigns of Owner and Farm in like manner as on the original parties, unless modified by mutual agreement.

21. The parties agree that this Agreement shall be governed by the laws of the State of ________________________.

IN WITNESS WHEREOF, the parties have executed this lease at ______________________________________, on the date first above written.

FARM

OWNER_________________________ By:__________________________

Certificate of Breeding

A certificate of breeding is usually issued by the breeding farm at the time a mare is picked up from the farm after breeding to the stallion. It specifies the stallion to which the mare was bred and the dates the breedings occurred. It can then be used to assist the mare owner and the treating veterinarian in determining the actual conception date and gestation period for a foal after the mare has been pronounced "in foal."

Certificate of Breeding

I, ______________________________, owner of the stallion named ____________________________________, and described as follows: ____, hereby certify and warrant that said stallion bred the mare named
(Age, Color, Breed)
___________________________, and owned by ______________________ ___________________________ Registration Number _________________ described as ____ on
(Age, Color, Breed)
the following dates and times:

Date_______________ Time_______________

Date_______________ Time_______________

Date_______________ Time_______________

Date_______________ Time_______________

I hereby agree to execute all necessary registration papers for any foal(s) both of said described breedings and should I fail to do so I appoint ________________________________ as my agent who is authorized hereby to execute said necessary papers based on the information set forth herein.

EXECUTED this _____________ day of ___________, 19_____ at _______________________.

____
(Stallion Owner)

____
(Address)

(Note: This agency appointment may or may not be accepted by the individual registry. One should check with the Breed Registry in question to determine if the above agency will be accepted should for some reason the owner fail to execute said registration papers.)

Agreement for Lease of Mare

Where a mare is leased for breeding purposes, an agreement for the lease of said mare is essential. This is very different from a simple lease of a mare for riding purposes. Normally, the lessee (the party who is leasing the mare) in such a lease agreement is authorized by the lessor (the actual owner of the mare) to use the mare for breeding purposes only.

The terms for the lease of a mare for breeding purposes can and often do vary depending on the needs of the parties. Usually, the owner of the mare (Lessor) maintains ownership of the mare while the party leasing the mare (Lessee) will be responsible for all costs and expenses attenuant to the mare for the term of the lease, as wen as any additional costs called for under the lease agreement. However, normally the Lessee will be the sole owner of any foal resulting from the actual breeding of the mare.

The actual breed of the mare, i.e. thoroughbred, standardbred, arabian, etc. has no substantial significance under this type of lease agreement, as long as the mare is to be used primarily for breeding purposes.

Agreement for Lease of Mare

THIS AGREEMENT entered into this ____________________ day of ________________, 19 ____, by and between ____________________ ________________________ hereinafter referred to as "Lessor" and ____ hereinafter referred to as "Lessee".

Lessor hereby leases to Lessee, who is engaged in the business of breeding ____________________ (Breed) horses, the following horse: ______________________________________ (Name of Horse) a ________________ (Age), ___________________ (Color), _____________________ (Breed), mare for breeding purposes by Lessee.

I. TERM

The term of this lease shall be for approximately ________________ (__________) months, beginning ________________ and ending when the foal to be received by Lessee herein has been weaned. Should Lessor leave the mare with Lessee beyond the term of this lease, then Lessor shall pay the sum of $__________________ per day for feed and board to Lessee, plus necessary veterinary and blacksmith costs, after at least three (3) days written notice from Lessee that the mare is ready to be returned to Lessor.

II. LEASE PAYMENTS

In consideration of the rights and benefits received hereunder, Lessee agrees to pay the Lessor the following sums:

$____________________ to be paid when said mare is pronounced in foal:

$____________________ on or before _________________, 19_____. Provided, however, if mare does not come into foal by _______________, 19____, Lessee, at his option, may continue the lease on the same basis in 19______ with no additional lease payments over and above those noted above, or he may terminate this lease and return said mare to Lessor and Lessee shall assume the costs of maintenance to date of termination as agreed to in Paragraph III.

If the mare is pronounced in foal, but a live foal is not born to said mare for any reason whatsoever, Lessee may, at his option, renew this lease on the same terms in 19____, without additional lease payments, or in the alternative, terminate the lease and all monies paid shall be refunded to Lessee. However, in either case Lessee shall assume the cost of maintenance to date as provided in Paragraph III. "Live Foal" as used herein shall mean the foal has stood and nursed from a mare or has been fed by hand, in each case for at least a period of 24 hours.

III. CARE AND MAINTENANCE

As further consideration to Lessor hereunder, Lessee covenants that he shall assume the full care and maintenance of Lessor's horse during the term of this lease and agrees to provide reasonable breeding conditions and facilities, furnish proper feed, sufficient water, farrier care, adequate shelter, exercise, medical and veterinary care as required, in a manner consistent with good horse breeding practices in the State of _________________ at Lessee's own expense as determined by Lessee. However after Lessor has received the three (3) day notice described in paragraph I, Lessor shall assume all the costs related to such mare.

IV. USES

Lessor is authorized to use such mare for breeding purposes only.

V. SUBLEASE: ASSIGNMENT

Lessee shall not assign this lease, or any interest herein, nor sublet any mare or filly or in any manner permit the use of Lessor's horse for any purpose other than herein set forth.

VI. RISK OF LOSS

Lessor shall bear all risk of loss from the death or harm to any of its horses unless such loss is caused by the gross negligence of Lessee, its agents or employees, in which case Lessee shall bear such loss. Lessee shall have no responsibility to maintain insurance on the life of the horse during the term of this lease.

VII. INDEMNITY

Lessee agrees that he will indemnify Lessor against, and hold Lessor and Lessor's horses free and harmless from all liens, encumbrances, charges and claims whether contractual or imposed by operation of law.

VIII. INSURANCE

Lessee shall, at his own expense, at all times during the term of this lease, maintain insurance for injury to or death of persons or loss or damages to their property occurring in or about the premises on which Lessor's horse shall be used for breeding. Such insurance shall provide for $___________ per injury, $_____________ per accident, and $_____________ property damage.

IX. PERMISSION TO INSPECT

Lessee shall permit inspection of the horse by Lessor at any and all reasonable times after reasonable notice of Lessor's intent to do so.

X. REMEDIES IN EVENT OF DEFAULT

If either party hereto shall default with respect to any material condition or covenant hereof, by him to be performed, the other party may, but need not, declare this Agreement to be terminated. The breaching party shall be responsible to the other for reasonable attorney's fees and court costs related to any breach.

XI. WAIVER

No delay or omission to exercise any right, power, or remedy accruing to either party on any breach or default of Lessee under this lease shall impair any such right, power, or remedy of said party, nor shall it be construed to be a waiver of any such breach or default, or an acquiescence therein, or in any similar breach or default thereafter occurring; nor shall any waiver of any single breach or default be deemed a waiver of any other breach or default theretofore or thereafter occurring. Any waiver, permit, or approval of any kind or character on the part of either party of any breach or default under this lease, or any waiver on part of the other party of any provision or condition of this lease, must be in writing and should be effective only to extent in such writing specifically set forth. All remedies, either under this lease or by law, or otherwise afforded to Lessor, shall be cumulative and not alternative.

XII. EFFECT OF LEASE

The provisions of this lease shall be binding on the heirs, executors, administrators and assigns of Lessor and Lessee in like manner as on the original parties, unless modified by mutual agreement.

XIII. GOVERNING LAW

The parties agree that this lease shall be governed by the laws of the State of ___________________.

IN WITNESS WHEREOF, the parties have executed this lease at ____ on the date first above written.

LESSOR:	LESSEE:
______________________ (Name)	______________________ (Name)
______________________ (Address)	______________________ (Address)
______________________	______________________
______________________ (Phone)	______________________ (Phone)

Stallion Lease Agreement

Very often, a breeding farm will lease a stallion it otherwise has no financial interest in from a third party to stand at its farm. In such a case, a stallion lease agreement is important to lay out the responsibilities between the farm and the stallion owner. The number of mares to be bred (total book) should be set forth in the stallion lease agreement, as well as any free breeding rights that the farm, or for that matter any other party, is to receive under a normal book of mares.

There is no set rule for who is to receive free breeding rights, if any. Normally the breeding farm may reserve a number of free breeding rights as part of its consideration for standing the stallion. In addition, breeding rights have been known to be designated for third parties such as trainers and treating veterinarians for their past and/or present services with regard to the horse, in recognition of that person's role in the success of the horse as a racehorse or sporthorse, or whatever the case may be. The owner of the stallion may also be given free breeding rights as part of his consideration for allowing the farm to lease the stallion.

The terms of the stallion lease agreement can vary but should include how the profits from any breedings sold as outside bookings are to be disbursed between the parties. Do the Lessor (Owner of the Stallion) and Lessee (Breeding Farm) split the net profits from any and all breedings to outside mares on a 50/50 split, or is there some other arrangement made? Certainly the breeding fee being charged and the number of outside mares permitted to be bred are the main considerations here. For example, thoroughbred horses by Jockey Club rules and regulations must be bred by natural cover and, therefore, are more limited in the number of bookings to mares (normally 40-45 total book). Standardbred stallions, on the other hand, are permitted under the rules and regulations of the United States Trotting Association to be bred by artificial insemination and, therefore, are capable of breeding a more substantial number of mares in any particular breeding season (i.e. 120-150 mares as a total book is not uncommon).

The breeding farm is nominally responsible for the care, board and maintenance of the stallion under the lease agreement, as well for any advertising and/or promotion that may be required to properly promote the stallion. Often, a minimum advertising or promotion budget is stated in any lease agreement in order that the Lessor (Owner of the Stallion) is guaranteed a certain amount of exposure of the stallion by the breeding farm as part and parcel of his agreement to lease the stallion to the breeding farm.

All the terms and conditions noted above and more can be properly negotiated by the parties or through their teamed counsel. The important thing to note here is that nothing is set in stone. Whatever the parties can mutually agree to will be enough to create a proper lease agreement and to hold the agreement legally binding.

Stallion Lease Agreement

THIS AGREEMENT is entered into on this ______________ day of ____________________, 19____ by and between __________________ ________________________________, residing at ________________ ____ owner(s) of the
(Address)
________________, _____________, ________________ stallion,
(Age) (Color) (Breed)
to-wit: _____________________________, ____________________
(Name of Stallion) (Registration #)
hereinafter referred to as "lessor"; and, residing at ____ hereinafter
(Address)
referred to as "lessee", on the following terms and conditions:

1. Lessor agrees to lease the stallion, ______________________
(Name of Stallion)
______________________________ hereinafter referred to as "Stallion:, to Lessee for the period of time from _____________, 19____ to ________________. 19____, for the consideration of $_____________ payable in __________ (__________) installments of $________________ for the purpose of breeding mares owned by Lessee and/or other third parties.

2. Lessee agrees to insure said stallion for the period of ________________ with mortality insurance purchased through the _________________________________ for a sum $____________,
(Insurance Company or Agency)
said insurance payable to Lessor as beneficiary. Lessee agrees to reimburse Lessor for the premium necessary for such insurance upon receipt of copy of the invoice.

3. Lessee will be responsible for the expense of suitable transportation of stallion from the stable of Lessor to the stable of the Lessee and back to the stable of Lessor at the termination of this Agreement. Such transportation shall be selected and designated at the Lessor's discretion.

4. Lessee shall, at all times during the term of this Agreement, at his expense, provide adequate feed, water, shelter, care and maintenance and veterinary attention to the horse described above in accordance with good husbandry, including routine injections for the prevention of disease and routine medication for the suppression of internal parasites. Lessee will be responsible for the services of a farrier to keep stallion shod on a regular basis. Lessee will furnish to Lessor, at least every sixty (60) days a written report of all breedings performed by stallion.

5. It is understood that, during the year of 19____ Lessee may, at his discretion, breed mares charging stud fees of not less than $________________, with the Lessor to receive payment of $_____________ per outside mare bred. Lessee agrees to pay to Lessor $ _____________ within 10 days of each payment by mare owner of such amount. Payments not made to same within ten (10) days shall accrue interest on the unpaid balance at the rate of twelve (12%) percent per annum. It is further understood that Lessee may, at his discretion, advertise the said stallion as standing at ____________________________________.
(Farm Name)
Lessee may also breed ____________________ (______________) mares
(Number Spelled) (Numeral)
belonging to himself and others designated by the Lessee on the attached Schedule "A" to this Agreement, at no cost to the Lessee. However, the book must be closed at not more than __________________ (__________) mares for the lease period.
(Number Spelled) (Numeral)

6. Lessor agrees to execute, on request of the Lessee and on presentation of evidence that such breedings were made, the Stallion Report for 19____ on stallion which is required by the __________________________ by ___________________, 19____, and
(Breed Registry)
further, to sign all breeding certificates duly executed as

stated in item 5 above. Lessor only, shall have the right to sign said documents, unless otherwise agreed by Lessor, in writing.

7. Live Foal Guarantees or Breed Back Rights: Lessor shall assume only the following responsibility for re-breeding a mare upon return to Lessor of said stallion, and Lessee agrees to have only the following foal guarantee terms in Lessee's breeding contracts:

(a) Should a mare be not declared in foal by the end of forty-five (45) days from the last breeding of said mare, Lessee of the stallion agrees to re-breed said mare at any time, provided however, if after ______________________, 19____, the mare owner may have the re-breeding performed in the breeding season of 19____. Should the mare not become in foal after the re-breeding, then the stallion Lessor or Lessee shall have no further re-breeding obligation.

(b) Should the mare be declared in foal and not have a live foal, which is defined as standing and feeding from the mare or standing and being fed, then the Lessee shall agree to rebreed the mare during the 19____ breeding season.

(c) The owner of the mare shall have no further rights of breeding or re-breeding, or further rights to a live foal after such breeding.

8. It is hereby understood and agreed by and between the parties of this Agreement that Lessor retains the privilege of having ____________________ (Number Spelled) (__________) (Numeral) ______________________ (Breed) mares bred to stallion during the term of this Agreement, with Lessee receiving no fee for such breedings except customary board for the care of such mares while at ________________ (Farm Name) ____________________________________.

9. Lessor agrees that Lessee shall have the option to lease said Stallion, ______________________________, for the year
(Name of Stallion)
19____, on the same terms and conditions as hereinabove agreed to, with an additional $______________________ paid by __________________, 19_____. It is further agreed that Lessee must give Lessor at least ninety (90) days prior written notice of their intent to exercise said option. Failure to meet the timely notice necessary to exercise said option, the requirements thereof or the payment of the additional $__________________ shall give Lessor the right to terminate this lease as of _____________, 19____.

10. This Agreement may be terminated on the basis of any of the following reasons upon ten (10) days written notice:

a) By mutual agreement of Lessor and Lessee;

b) By Lessor for failure of Lessee to pay the consideration as hereinabove described within 10 days when due;

c) By Lessor, if, in the opinion of the Lessor, the stallion is not receiving proper care;

d) By Lessee, if upon presentation of evidence from a doctor of veterinary medicine, the horse was found to be impotent or not able to perform breeding for any physical condition. If such occurs, Lessee shall have no right to a refund of any monies paid and the $__________ must be paid by Lessee irrespective of any such conditions occurring to the stallion; and,

e) For a material breach of the terms set forth herein.

11. All terms and covenants of this Agreement shall be enforced and construed in accordance with the laws of the State of ______________________________.

12. Should either party breach this Agreement, the breaching party agrees to pay the other party reasonable attorney's fees and court costs incurred as a result of such breach.

IN WITNESS WHEREOF, the parties hereto have executed this Lease Agreement as of the day and year first above written.

LESSOR:	LESSEE:
______________________________	______________________________
______________________________	______________________________

OWNER(S) OF:

____
Name of Stallion

____
Registration #

Training Agreement

Any professional horse trainer would benefit from having a written training agreement setting forth the basic terms and conditions, including fees, from which he earns his livelihood. These terms, conditions and fees as set forth will, of course, vary depending on the type of trainer the professional horseman might be. For example, a professional racehorse trainer, whether he be in the Thoroughbred, Standardbred, Quarterhorse or Arabian industries will get paid usually substantially different than, for example, a hunter-jumper trainer, dressage trainer, or reining or cutting trainer.

The racehorse trainer often gets enough monthly fees to cover the basic training costs for a horse, but normally very little profit is computed in these basic training fees, as a professional racehorse trainer is expected to earn most of his money by winning purses. As a result, a designated percentage of the winnings of his charges on the basis of their racing performance to the trainer is very common. On the other hand, a show horse trainer does not normally compete for the same type of money available in racing, and therefore, he or she must receive his or her remuneration based on a different scale of performance. Therefore, a show horse's remuneration is often based on a different percentage of earnings than that might be prevalent in the racehorse industry.

In addition to the above, the rules of racing and the various racing jurisdictions may have some bearing on the terms, conditions and fees (i.e. the percentage of earnings due to the trainer), as will the rules and regulations under the American Horse Show Association, where applicable. A licensed racehorse trainer is deemed held responsible and have to full knowledge of the rules and regulations in those states where he or she is licensed, as also is any recognized trainer with the AHSA.

The sample training agreements set forth here were developed specifically with the differences noted above in mind. Either one of the agreements presented may prove more useful with regard to the specific use and type of training involved. Again, nothing is set in stone, and any written agreement mutually agreed to by the parties can be better enforced and, therefore, of more benefit than no written agreement at all.

Training Agreement

Agreement made ______________________________, 19____ between ______________________________________, residing at ____________ ____ herein called "Owner", and ______________________________________ residing at ____ herein called "Trainer".

Owner is the legal owner of __________________________ certain thoroughbred horses described below bred for racing and is desirous of having these horses trained and raced. Trainer is a thoroughbred racehorse trainer and desirous of training and racing these horses.

In consideration of the covenants and agreements herein set forth, the parties agree as follows:

I. DESCRIPTION AND DELIVERY OF HORSES

Owner agrees to deliver the following horses to trainer to trainer to be trained and raced at ______________________________ [or in race tracks throughout the State of ______________________ as the case may be]:

Name of Horse	Age	Color & Sex	Jockey Club Registration No.
____________________	_____	________________	________________
____________________	_____	________________	________________

II. PAYMENT FOR TRAINING

Owner agrees to pay Trainer ________________________ ($__________) Dollars per day per horses trained and/or raced, subject to

the provisions of Section Six. This daily charge shall be payable on or before the ____________ day of each month.

III. DUTIES OF TRAINER

Trainer shall train and race the horses and feed and care for them, subject to Section Four herein, in a manner consistent with accepted horsetraining practices in the State of _________________________. Trainer, in his sole discretion, shall decide when any of owner's horses are sufficiently trained to be entered in a race, and Trainer has sole discretion to decide what type of race any horse may be entered in and how often each horse should be raced, except that Trainer shall not enter any of Owner's horses in any claiming race for the sum of ________________ ($________) Dollars or less without prior consent of Owner.

IV. EXPENSES

Owner shall bear the cost of transporting the horses from one track to another or otherwise, veterinary and medical costs, costs of preparation of racing silks, jockey fees, pony leads and/or any costs of equipment that Trainer may deem necessary to the proper training and racing of any of owner's horses, in addition to insurance costs as set forth in Section Ten below.

V. ACCOUNTING AND BILLING BY TRAINER

Trainer shall pay all expenses referred to in Section Four, keep an accurate account thereof, and bill Owner for the same at the end of each month. If owner fails to reimburse Trainer for such expenses when payable, Trainer is authorized to deduct an amount equal to such expenses from owner's account from the

Horsemen's Bookkeeper at the race track where Owner's horses are being trained and raced, pursuant to the limited power of attorney set forth in connection with this agreement and incorporated herein by reference.

VI. OTHER COMPENSATION TO TRAINER AND JOCKEY

In the event any of Owner's horses win a race, owner shall cause to be deducted from owner's share of the purse money therefrom, ten per cent (10%), which amount is to be paid to Trainer over and above any other compensation provided for herein. In addition, Owner shall deduct ten per cent (10%) from such purse money and cause the same to be paid to the jockey riding Owner's horse in the winning race, in addition to regular jockey fees. No deductions from any other money awarded to Owner for any other finishing position of Owner's horses, shall be deducted from such purses and paid as additional compensation to Trainer or jockey other than the regular jockey mount fees.

VII. HORSES OUT OF TRAINING

If, during the term of this Agreement, any of Owner's horses are taken out of training after being put into training, Owner shall pay the costs of boarding, feeding, veterinarian services and medicine, and transportation in maintaining any such horse, but shall not pay Trainer compensation for training as hereinabove set forth. Trainer shall notify Owner as soon as it is known that horse is or has been removed from training, and Owner shall pay thereafter ________________ ($___________) Dollars per day until the horse can be returned to training or can no longer remain at the track.

VIII. AMENDMENT OF AGREEMENT

This Agreement may be amended at any time by writing into the provisions herein set forth, the description of any additional racing stock desired by both parties to be placed within the terms of this Agreement, and the amendment shall be initialed by both parties hereto.

IX. DURATION AND TERMINATION OF AGREEMENT

The term of this Agreement shall be for ________________________ commencing _____________, 19____ and terminating ______________, 19____. Either party hereto may cancel this Agreement on five (5) days written notice to the other party provided all funds owing to Trainer shall be paid prior to Owner taking possession of said horse(s) . Both parties may renew this Agreement for the term hereof on written agreement by the other party hereto.

X. INSURANCE AND IDENTIFICATION

a) Insurance. Upon receipt of the horses herein described, Trainer shall procure thoroughbred race horse insurance protecting Owner against any losses due to fire, theft, death, or other disability arising from any injuries of accidents to said horses, such insurance to provide coverage in an amount not less than _____________ ($__________) Dollars. Owner agrees to reimburse Trainer for such insurance costs in the manner set forth in Section Five above.

b) Indemnity. Trainer agrees to indemnify Owner from all liability or claims, demands, damages and costs for or arising out of the training and racing of Owner's horses, whether it be caused by the negligence of Trainer, his agents or employees, or otherwise.

XI. RACING NAME

Owner's horses shall be raced in the name of ____________________ ____________________, as Owner, and ____________________, as Trainer. Trainer shall not enter any of Owner's horses in any race in which Trainer has another horse in his barn that is to be entered in the same race, without prior written consent from Owner.

XII. EFFECT OF TERMINATION OF AGREEMENT

If this Agreement is terminated for any reason prior to the expiration thereof, Trainer shall immediately deliver any horses under this Agreement to Owner.

DATED:____________________

____
Trainer

____
(Address)

____

____
Owner

____
(Address)

____

Training Agreement for

____

THIS AGREEMENT is entered into this ________________ day of ____________, 19____ by and between ______________________ (Name) ____________________ of ______________________ (Address) ______________________________ hereinafter referred to as "Owner", and ______________________________ (Training Stable), hereinafter referred to as "TRAINER".

WHEREAS, OWNER owns/leases the below described horses and desires TRAINER to train said horses for the purposes set forth herein; and

WHEREAS, the parties desire to agree on the terms and conditions of such training.

NOW, THEREFORE, it is hereby agreed as follows:

1. Description and Delivery of Horses

OWNER agrees to deliver, on or about ________________ the following described horse(s) to TRAINER:

NAME **AGE** **COLOR** **SEX** **REG. NO** (if applicable)

(a) ______________________________

(b) ______________________________

(c) ______________________________

(d) ______________________________

2. Payment for Training

OWNER agrees to pay TRAINER the sum of $________________ per day per head of horses trained subject to the terms and

conditions hereof. Said charge shall be payable on or before the first of each month and any payment not received by TRAINER by the fifth of the each month shall incur additional interest at twelve 12% percent per annum for the number of days past the first of the month that the payment is delinquent. Further, if the payment is not received by the fifteenth of each month, an additional TEN DOLLAR ($10.00) handling charge shall be added to the monthly charge as indicated above.

3. Duties of Trainer

TRAINER agrees to perform the following in a manner consistent with industry practices: [List specific duties, if any]

(a) ____________________

(b) ____________________

(c) ____________________

(d) ____________________

4. Expenses

OWNER shall bear all costs of all transportation incidental to the purposes of this Agreement, including, but not limited to, veterinary and medical costs, entry fees, special equipment needed on an emergency basis that the TRAINER may deem necessary to the proper showing of any of OWNER'S horses's; however, such expenses shall not exceed $____________________ without OWNER'S prior approval. Payment terms shall be in accordance with paragraph 2 above.

5. Accounting and Billing by Trainer

TRAINER shall pay all expenses referred to in Paragraph 4, keep an accurate account thereof, and bill OWNER for the same at the end of each month. If OWNER fails to reimburse TRAINER

for such expenses when payable, TRAINER is authorized to deduct an amount equal to such expenses from OWNER'S account, if any, held by TRAINER from show winnings, or any other source available to TRAINER.

6. Other Compensation to Trainer and Rider (optional)

In the event any of OWNER'S horses win a class with prize money entered and shown by the TRAINER or an authorized rider, OWNER shall pay TRAINER __________% of said prize money, which amount is to be paid to TRAINER over and above any other compensation provided for herein. TRAINER shall have no right to any other prize money.

7. Horses Out of Training

If, during the term of this Agreement, any of OWNER'S horses are taken out of training for an extended period, OWNER shall pay the costs of board and feed at the rate of $___________ per day, veterinarian services and medicine, and transportation in maintaining any such horse, but shall not pay TRAINER compensation for training as hereinabove set forth. TRAINER shall advise OWNER of such taking out of training within three (3) days thereof.

8. Term and Termination of Agreement

The term of this Agreement shall be for ______________ months, commencing on ____________________, 19_____ and terminating on ____________________, 19______ (or can be on a month-to-month basis), or upon three (3) days' written notice to the other party and a final accounting thereto based on a daily pro rata basis shall be prepared by TRAINER and any amounts due shall be paid by OWNER within five (5) days, provided all funds owing

to TRAINER shall be paid prior to OWNER taking possession of said horse(s).

9. Board and Feed

TRAINER shall provide the following described care and feed:

Stall: (minimum size____________________)

Paddock or Turnout:____________________

Feed: (1)_______lbs _______hay, _______times daily

(2)_______lbs _______grain, _______times daily

(3) other:______________________________________

____

10. Insurance and Indemnification

A. Insurance. [Optional but recommended.] Prior to receipt of the horses herein described, TRAINER shall have procured appropriate care, custody and control insurance protecting OWNER against any losses due to fire, theft, death or other disability arising from any injuries or accidents to said horses caused by negligence of TRAINER, his agents, or employees, including during transportation thereof, such insurance to provide coverage in an amount not less than $______________. OWNER agrees to reimburse TRAINER not less than $______________ of said premium for said insurance. OWNER agrees to reimburse TRAINER for such insurance costs in the manner set forth in Paragraphs 4 and 5 above [or TRAINER shall carry no care, custody and control insurance on the horses above listed]. TRAINER agrees to maintain liability insurance in the sum of $_________________ each person, $______________ each accident, and $___________________ property damage.

TRAINER will make available to OWNER, upon request, proof of such above described insurance as being in force.

b. Indemnity. Except as covered by insurance provided, OWNER agrees to indemnify TRAINER from all liability or claims, demands, damages and costs for or arising out of the breaking, training and showing of OWNER'S horses, whether it be caused by the negligence of TRAINER, his agents or employees, or otherwise.

11. Showing Name

OWNER'S horses shall be shown in the name of ______________________ ____________________, as OWNER, and ____________________________________ _______________________, as TRAINER.

12. Effect of Termination of Agreement

If this Agreement is terminated for any reason prior to the expiration thereof, TRAINER shall immediately deliver any horse(s) under this Agreement to OWNER. OWNER understands, however, TRAINER has a lien pursuant to ___________________________ (State) law and may demand payment in full prior to releasing said horses.

13. Authority to Obtain veterinary and Farrier Care

OWNER hereby authorizes TRAINER to obtain all necessary emergency veterinary and non-emergency farrier care to maintain said animal(s) in good health. All other non-emergency care needs shall be first approved by OWNER unless otherwise authorized hereunder. OWNER shall pay all such veterinarian and farrier services in accordance with Paragraphs 4 and 5 above.

14. Binding Effect on Successors/Attorney Fees: Law

A. This Agreement shall be binding upon the assigns, heirs, executors and administrators of the respective parties.

B. Should either party breach this Agreement, the breaching party agrees to pay the other's reasonable attorney fees and court costs related to such breach.

C. This Agreement shall be interpreted and construed in accordance with the laws of the State of ____________________.

15. Amendments

This Agreement may be amended at any time by writing, into the provisions herein set forth, and the description of any additional horse(s) desired by both parties to be placed within the terms of the Agreement, and the amendment shall be initialled by both parties hereto.

IN WITNESS WHEREOF, the parties have executed this Agreement at ______________________________ on the day and year first above written.

	TRAINING STABLE:
______________________________ Owner	By: ______________________________ Trainer
______________________________ Address	______________________________ Address
______________________________	______________________________
______________________________ Telephone No.	______________________________ Telephone No.

Lease Agreement for a Performance Horse

Lease Agreements for the use of performance horses have become more and more prevalent over the years. In normal cases, one party simply agrees to lease a particular horse for a specific period of time and for a specific purpose while normally being responsible for any and all expenses and costs incurred for the maintaining and training of the horse during said time period. Instead of purchasing the horse, a lessee will often pay a monthly or annual fee for the lease of the horse.

Sometimes part of the lease agreement will involve distribution of any purses or monies earned in a previously agreed manner. Anotherwards, in lieu of the actual lease payments, the Lessor (Owner of the horse) will receive a percentage of any purse earnings by the subject horse.

One other point of importance here. Often there will be an option to purchase in the lease agreement whereby the Lessee will have the option to purchase the horse being leased at a certain predetermined price during the term of the lease agreement or at the end of the lease period. The amount of the purchase price should be prenegotiated in order that the option can be enforced, provided all the other terms and conditions of the contract are met by the parties. If for any reason the option price cannot be predetermined, there should be a formula specifically designated and used for determining how the price is to be determined at a later date; This will protect both parties and hopefully prevent any dispute as to how the option purchase price is to be determined at a future date.

Lease Agreement

THIS AGREEMENT is entered into between ______________________ ______________________ residing at ______________________ ______________________, hereinafter referred to as "LESSOR", and ______________________ residing at ______________________ hereinafter referred to as "LESSEE";

A. TERMS OF LEASE

This lease shall commence on ______________________ and terminate on ______________________ for a period of ______________________ (months) and covers the horse(s) described in paragraph B below.

B. DESCRIPTION

a) Name: ______________________

b) Age: ______________________

c) Breed: ______________________

d) Sex: ______________________

e) Registration No: ______________________

C. OPTION

Lessee has the option to renew this lease for an additional ____________ months by advising Lessor in writing at any time prior to ninety (90) days prior to the expiration of this lease.

At the expiration of said lease, and up to ______________ months thereafter, if Lessor places the horse up for sale, the Lessee shall have the first option to purchase the horse for ______________ ($__________) Dollars.

D. RENTAL FEE

In consideration of this lease, Lessee agrees to pay Lessor the following sum(s) on the date(s) indicated below:

____

____

E. EXERCISE

Lessee shall provide the following exercise of said horse(s) at the frequency and time period indicated below:

F. PURPOSE

Lessee is leasing said horse(s) for: ___________________________

____ and Les-
(Describe purposes)
sor warrants that said horse(s) are fit for said purpose(s).

G. SPECIAL RIGHTS OF LESSEE

(e.g. Lessee agrees not to sublease said horse to any other party, nor allow horse to be shown by any other party).

H. SPECIAL INSTRUCTIONS

(Describe special care required for animal, treatment, bedding, blanketing, etc.)

I. RISK OF LOSS

Lessee hereby assumes risk of loss or injury to said horse(s) except where caused by negligence of Lessor. Lessee agrees to purchase full horse mortality insurance on horse in amount of $_______________ covering the terms of said lease and naming the Lessor as sole beneficiary.

J. HOLD HARMLESS

Lessee hereby agrees to hold Lessor harmless from and against any and all claims, actions, damages, liability and expense in connection with loss of life, personal injury and/ or damage to property arising out of the use or care of the subject horse.

K. OWNERSHIP REGISTRATION

Lessor warrants that he has good and clear title to said horse(s) free from any liens.

L. TRANSPORTATION

Lessee (Lessor) shall assume all transportation costs relating to the leasing of said horse(s) hereunder.

M. FEED AND FACILITIES

Lessee agrees to feed and stable the horse(s) leased herein in accordance with the following;

Stall:_____________________
(minimum size)

Pasture or Turnout:_______________________

Grain: __________ pounds per day ____________ times per day

Hay: __________ pounds per day ____________ times per day

N. CARE

Lessee agrees to maintain said horse(s) in good health and to provide all necessary veterinarian and blacksmith needs at no cost to Lessor.

O. LIENS

Lessee agrees to keep said horse(s) free of all liens, encumbrances, charges and claims and Lessee agrees to hold Lessor harmless therefrom.

P. DEFAULT

Upon material breach of this Agreement by one party, the other party may terminate same.

On any breach, the other party shall have the right to recover from said breaching party all reasonable attorney's fees and court costs.

THIS AGREEMENT is subject to the laws of the State of ____________________________.

EXECUTED this ____________________ day of _________________, 19____, at __________________________, _________________________.
(State)

LESSOR	LESSEE
____________________ (name)	____________________ (name)
____________________ (address)	____________________ (address)
____________________	____________________
____________________ (phone)	____________________ (phone)

Consignment Agreement

Whenever an owner entrusts a professional horsemen to sell a horse on his or her behalf, it is sound business advice that a consignment agreement be drawn up between the parties to make sure that both parties are protected upon the sale of the horse.

The professional who is selling the horse is acting as an agent on behalf of the owner of the horse. As such, there are certain legal and fiduciary responsibilities and duties owed by the professional to the owner of the horse. "Fiduciary" is a term derived from the Roman law and means a person holding the character of a trustee, or a character analogous to that of a trustee, in respect to the trust and confidence involved in it and the scrupulous good faith and candor it requires. Thus a person is a fiduciary who is invested with rights and powers to be exercised for the benefit of another person. One is said to act in a "fiduciary capacity" or to receive money, or contract a debt in a "fiduciary capacity", when the business which he handles is not his own or for his benefit, but for the benefit of another person, as to whom stands in a relation implying and necessitating great confidence and trust on the one part and a high degree of good faith on the other part.

The professional or person selling the horse on behalf of the owner is thereby given certain rights to act on behalf of the owner with regard to the sale, and also to receive and distribute the sale proceeds pertaining thereto, resulting in the "fiduciary" relationship described above.

The owner is the "principal" and the professional selling the horse is the recognized "agent" throughout the arrangement. The terms of the relationship between the principal and agent should be fully described in the consignment agreement, including but not limited to a minimum price acceptable to the owner for the sale of the horse. Also, as included in the consignment agreement form herein, there should be a "limited" power of attorney given to the professional for the purpose of effecting the sale of the horse. Any broader power of attorney is inappropriate and is not advised without the prior consent and approval of the owner's attorney or counsel.

It should be remembered that the consignment agreement is a contract between the principal (owner) and the agent (professional horseman). The terms within that agreement need not be disclosed to any third party or potential purchaser of the subject horse unless otherwise requested. However, once again, the limited power of attorney described above must be part of the consignment agreement and should be construed to be strictly "limited" to the transaction involving the sale of the horse. It is foreseeable that a potential purchaser might wish to see this "limited power of attorney" before pursuing the purchase of the horse with the agent. In such case, a separate document entitled "Certificate of Limited Power of Attorney" should be prepared and executed by the parties for review by interested third parties.

Consignment Agreement for the Sale of Horse

This Agreement is entered into between ______________________________
______________________________ residing at ______________________________
____ hereinafter referred
to as "Consignor", and ____
residing at ____
____ hereinafter referred to
as "Consignee".

WHEREAS, Consignor owns a ____________ (age), ____________ (color), ____________ (breed), ____________ (sex), ____________ (registration #) (if applicable); and

WHEREAS, Consignee is in the business of acting as agent in the purchase and sale of horses; and

WHEREAS, Consignor would like to sell the above named horse through Consignee; and

WHEREAS, Consignee would like to sell said horse on behalf of Consignor, it is hereby agreed as follows:

1. Consignor agrees to accept and Consignee agrees to sell said horse for a minimum selling price of $____________________ (Number Spelled) ($____________________ (Numeral)) under the following terms:

2. Board will be paid by Consignor to Consignee in the amount of $________________ per month until horse is sold or this Agreement is terminated.

3. Any variation to above terms must be approved by both parties in writing.

4. It is hereby agreed that Consignee shall receive a commission of ____________________% of all funds received with regard to the sale of said horse. Consignor shall receive the balance of all funds within 10 days of receipt of said funds by the Consignee. A late charge of % per month shall be applied to any late payment from Consignee to Consignor.

5. Care of Horse:

Consignee shall maintain said horse in accordance with good animal husbandry practices in the area. (eg. The horse shall be stabled and blanketed every evening when necessary and groomed daily to maintain good condition.) Consignee is authorized to obtain necessary veterinary and farrier care at Consignor's cost and expense. Such costs may be billed to Consignor directly.

6. Feeding Instructions:

The following feed and supplements shall be fed to said horse daily:

Hay: ___________ lbs ___________times daily

Grain: _________ lbs ___________times daily

7. Exercise:

The horse may be ridden by Consignee or a competent rider employed by Consignee and Consignee may present and otherwise show the horse to potential buyers under the following terms and conditions:

8. Delivery of Horse:

When sold, the horse shall be sold F.O.B. Consignee's farm and risk of loss shall pass upon delivery of registration papers and/or bill of sale to Buyer. Buyer shall assume all costs thereafter. Possession shall be given only upon receipt of consideration in accordance with the terms above or as otherwise agreed by Consignor in writing.

9. Lien:

Consignee shall keep said horse free and clear of liens and encumbrances while it is in Consignee's possession.

10. Power of Attorney:

Consignor hereby makes, constitutes, and appoints Consignee as his true and lawful Attorney with exclusive rights to sell Consignor's horse under the terms and conditions above described and for the express purpose of effecting the sale of said horse.

11. Attorney's Fees:

Should either party breach this Agreement, the other party shall have the right to receive from said breaching party attorney's fees and court costs related to such breach.

12. Termination:

This Agreement may be terminated by either party prior to sale of said horse upon five days written notice to the other provided all expenses for board of said horse are paid prior to the removal of said horse.

13. Applicable Law:

This Agreement will be subject to and under laws of the State of______________________________.

Dated:______________________ Consignor________________________________

Dated:______________________ Consignee________________________________

Limited Power of Attorney

KNOW ALL MEN BY THESE PRESENTS THAT, I,
____, residing at
(Name of Seller)
____,
____________________, ________________________, do, make,
(County) (State)
constitute and appoint ________________________________
(Name of Agent)
true and lawful Attorney for me in my name to act on my behalf in any and all matters concerning the sale of the horse described below herein, with full power to execute and transact matters and documents relating to said property, and to act in my behalf concerning all financial matters relating to said horse.

Name of Horse: ______________________________

Age: ____________________________________

Breed: __________________________________

Sex: ____________________________________

Size: ____________________________________

Registration No: ______________________________

IN WITNESS WHEREOF, I hereunto set my hand and seal this ________________ day of ____________, 19____.

____
Name of Seller

This ____________________ day of ____________, 19____. personally appeared before me, __________________ the above named ____________________________, and acknowledged the foregoing Power of Attorney to be act and deed and desired the same might be recorded as such, according to law.

WITNESS my hand and seal the day and year last above written.

____
NOTARY PUBLIC

Purchase and Sale Agreement

Even when the purchase price of a horse is paid in full at the time of the sale of a horse, it is prudent and wise that a purchase and sale agreement be executed in order to protect the parties. When the purchase price of the horse is to paid over time, i.e. in installment payments, it is absolutely essential that a purchase and sale agreement be executed by the parties.

A "cash" sale refers to the type of situation where a deposit is placed on the horse and the horse is to be paid for in full before the horse is actually permitted to leave the seller's premises. Normally, the horse, therefore, remains in the seller's possession until the sale is completed. The purpose of a "cash" sale and purchase agreement is basically to document the proposed sale of the horse under the terms and conditions outlined therein. It can be a fairly simple document, but it does help to protect the parties should a problem later arise, and there is a question of what was the basic understanding of the parties. For example, if the horse is being purchased for a particular purpose, and seller warrants that the horse is fit for that particular purpose, a written agreement documenting that fact would be of substantial importance if it turns out later that the buyer claims that the horse was not suitable for the purpose for which it was intended.

An "installment" agreement is where the buyer is purchasing a horse over time, and intends to make certain predetermined payments over a specified period or term. Normally in the cash deal, the horse is not released to the buyer until the horse is paid for in full. Therefore, the seller is assured of receiving payment before giving up possession of the horse.

It should also be pointed out here that there are different legal terms relating to the term "possession", in that there is what is defined as "actual" possession and what is defined as "constructive " possession. "Actual possession" is defined as the actual occupation or possession in fact, or possession which is clearly visible and open to the world. "Constructive possession" exists and is distinguished from actual possession where, although the property is not in the owner's possession, the owner maintains the right to demand, receive or recover the property by suit. This is important is two ways in our dealings with horses. First, in a cash purchase and sale agreement, often a horse is sent out on trial to a potential buyer prior to the horse being purchased by that buyer. In such a case, even though the potential buyer has "actual" possession of the horse, the owner or seller retains "constructive" possession of the horse, and therefore, has the right to demand the horse back at any time. Secondly, the use of "constructive" possession may come into play in installment payment situations.

Normally, in the installment sale situation, the buyer obtains and has possession of the horse during the time the horse is being paid off. The question is, who really owns the horse during this time? The answer is "it depends". A seller of a horse has several options in doing an installment agreement. One of those options is to set up the installment agreement whereby the installment agreement is executed and a UCC-1 Financing Statement is prepared and filed in the county or counties in which the seller and the buyer reside. This documents that the seller maintains a secured interest in the horse until the horse is paid for in full. In other words, the seller retains title in the horse and can sue to get the horse back at any time should buyer fail to make payments when due. In such a case, the seller has retained "constructive" possession of the horse even though the buyer has actual possession of the horse until the horse is paid for in full. Only after full payment has been made does title pass from the seller to the buyer. This can be further documented by the seller actually holding the registration papers for the horse until full payment is made.

However, as mentioned above, the seller has another option. That option under the installment agreement is for the seller to give the buyer actual and constructive possession of the horse by passing title to the buyer at settlement, or when the horse is picked up, and having the buyer sign a promissory note for the balance due. If the buyer fails to make the proper time payments when due, the note is called in default, and the seller can sue the buyer on the note immediately without demanding the horse back at all. It should be noted that by pursuing this option, a seller can obtain a judgment but is "unsecured" in that he or she retains no security or title in the horse in case the buyer simply has no money and cannot pay him. The advantage of this option is if the seller does not want the horse back, he can simply get a money judgment against the buyer. The question, of course, then becomes whether the seller can actually collect on the money judgment.

A third option, is more or less a combination of the two other options explained above, and is probably the one most recommended here. An installment agreement can be drafted which calls for the seller maintaining a secured interest in the horse as well as having the buyer sign a promissory note for the balance due at the time the possession of the horse is given to the buyer. The seller can retain title to the horse until the horse is paid for in full by holding the registration papers to the horse or by filing the UCC-1 Financing Statement. Thereby, if the buyer defaults on the installment payments, the seller remains a "secured" creditor and can sue the buyer to obtain the horse back. The seller must first repossess the horse, then attempt to re-sell the horse in order to mitigate his damages. If the horse is sold for less than the original purchase price the seller had with the original buyer, the seller can then sue the buyer under the installment agreement for the difference between the amount due under the promissory note and the amount that the seller actually received upon the re-sale of the horse.

If the reader thinks that this is all very complex, it is, and it is, therefore, highly recommended to the reader that he or she obtain experienced legal counsel to help prepare and/or review all documentation essential in an installment sale agreement.

Purchase and Sale Agreement
(Cash)

THIS AGREEMENT is made between ______________________________ ______________________ residing at ____________________________ ____ hereinafter referred to as "BUYER," and ____________________________________ residing at ____ ____, hereinafter referred to as "SELLER" for purchase and sale of the horse described below on the following terms and conditions of sale:

Name ______________________________________

Age _______________________________________

Color _____________________________________

Breed _____________________________________

Sex _______________________________________

Tattoo ____________________________________
(if applicable)

A. CONSIDERATION

In consideration of the total sum of $____________________, SELLER agrees to sell BUYER the horse described herein and BUYER agrees to buy said horse on the terms set forth herein.

B. PAYMENT TERMS

This purchase is for cash and BUYER agrees to pay $________________ as deposit on ______________________ (date) and the balance due of $______________ payable on __________________ (date).

C. WARRANTIES

(1) SELLER warrants that he has clear title to said horse.

(2) SELLER makes no other warranties, express or implied, including the warranties of fitness for a particular purpose except as may, be otherwise provided for in this Agreement.

(3) SELLER warrants the following:

(4) Should said horse fail to meet any of the above warranties at the time of delivery, provided same is discovered within __________________ days from date of delivery to BUYER, SELLER agrees to do the following:

D. REGISTRATION AND OWNERSHIP TRANSFERS

Upon payment in full, SELLER agrees to execute all necessary papers and to take all steps necessary to transfer ownership and registration of the animal to BUYER at no cost to BUYER.

E. RISK OF LOSS

Pending delivery to BUYER, SELLER shall assume the risk of loss of said horse and upon delivery, BUYER shall assume the risk of loss.

F. LAW

The terms of this Agreement and disputes developing thereunder shall be enforced and construed in accordance with the laws of the State of ___________________________.

G. DEFAULT

Upon material breach of this Agreement by one party, the other party may terminate same.

On any breach, the other party shall have the right to recover from said breaching party all reasonable attorney's fees and court costs.

EXECUTED this ____________________ day of ____________________, 19_____, at ____________________________________.
(state)

______________________________	______________________________
Seller	Buyer
______________________________	______________________________
Address	Address
______________________________	______________________________
______________________________	______________________________

Purchase and Sale Agreement
(Installment)

THIS AGREEMENT is made between ______________________________, residing at ____ ____ hereinafter referred to as "BUYER", and ___________________________________, residing at ____ hereinafter referred to as "SELLER";

This Agreement is entered into between BUYER and SELLER for purchase and sale of the horse described below on the following terms and conditions of sale:

Name ____

Age ____

Color ____

Breed ____

Sex ____

Tattoo # ____
(if applicable)

A. CONSIDERATION

Inconsideration of the total sum of $_______________________, SELLER agrees to sell BUYER the horse described herein and BUYER agrees to buy said horse on the terms set forth herein.

B. PAYMENT TERMS

Down payment of $______________________ due ___________________.

The balance of $___________________ shall be paid by BUYER over __________________ months with _____% interest on the unpaid balance. The first payment shall be due on ________________________

and all payments shall be due and owing on or prior to the ____________ day of each month thereafter.

A $______________ late charge shall be paid by BUYER for cash installment obligations over ____________ days late.

Should BUYER fail to make said payment, SELLER shall have the option to declare the balance of the note then owing to be due and payable.

C. SECURITY

To secure the payments and duties of this obligation, SELLER retains a security interest in said horse and BUYER agrees to execute a chattel mortgage and a UCC-1 Financing Statement.

(Note: Where a registered horse is being sold, the Seller retaining the registration papers until the horse is paid in full may be sufficient security as a chattel mortgage and, therefore, a UCC-1 financing statement may not be necessary.)

SELLER agrees and covenants to execute all necessary documents to record said security interest and should SELLER fail to execute said papers, it is hereby agreed that the signature on this Agreement shall be deemed to be equivalent to the execution of a chattel mortgage.

While a balance is owing under this Agreement:

(1) Buyer agrees not to remove said horse from ____________________________________, except where agreed
(County, State)
in writing by Seller.

(2) Buyer agrees to keep said horse in good health, and free from disease by providing adequate feed, shelter, veterinary care and blacksmith care.

(3) Buyer agrees to keep said horse free of all liens and encumbrances and to pay any and all taxes levied against such

horse when due.

Should Buyer default in any terms of this Agreement, Seller may foreclose on his security interest in any manner provided by law.

D. DELIVERY

Said Horse shall be delivered to BUYER and SELLER, F.O.B. ______________________________ on ____________.
(City or Town)

E. CARE.

Prior to delivery, SELLER shall have the duty to provide reasonable care of said horse including, but not limited to:

1. Feed
2. Exercise
3. Veterinarian
4. Blacksmith

SELLER is (authorized to) or (shall have the responsibility to) provide reasonable veterinary care at (Buyer) or (Seller) cost and (Buyer) or (Seller) agrees to indemnify (Buyer) or (Seller) for any costs incurred. [Cross out one.]

F. WARRANTIES:

(1) SELLER warrants that he has clear title to said horse.

(2) SELLER makes no other warranties express or implied, including the warranties of fitness for a particular purpose except as otherwise specified in this Agreement.

(3) SELLER warrants the following:

(4) Should said horse fail to meet any of the above warranties at the time of delivery, provided same is discovered within

_____________ days from date of delivery to BUYER, SELLER agrees to do the following:

G. REGISTRATION AND OWNERSHIP TRANSFERS

Upon payment in full, SELLER agrees to execute all necessary papers and to take all steps necessary to transfer ownership and registration of the animal to BUYER at no cost to BUYER.

H. RISK OF LOSS

Pending delivery to BUYER, SELLER shall assume the risk of loss of said horse and upon delivery, BUYER shall assume the risk of loss.

I. INSURANCE (Optional but recommended).

Pending delivery to BUYER, SELLER agrees to indemnify and hold BUYER harmless from any injury to any person or damage to property caused by said horse, and carry liability insurance to cover such liability with $_____________ personal injury and $__________ for damage to property and $______________ per accident and to name BUYER additional insured.

J. LAW

The terms of this Agreement and disputes developing thereunder shall be enforced and construed in accordance with the laws of the State of ___________________.

K. DEFAULT

Upon material breach of this Agreement by one party, the other party may terminate same.

On any breach, the other party shall have the right to recover from said breaching party all reasonable attorney's fees and court costs.

EXECUTED this ____________ day of ______________, 19____, at _______________________________, ___________________.

_________________________	_________________________
Seller	Buyer
_________________________	_________________________
Address	Address
_________________________	_________________________
_________________________	_________________________

Promissory Note

______________________________ (Total Amount of Note) ______________________________ (Date of Note)

FOR VALUE RECEIVED, ______________________________ (Debtor) promises to pay to the order of ______________________________ (Seller of Horse), ______________________ (Price of Horse) ($________________) Dollars, without offset, in one lump sum payment due on or before ________________ (Date payment due).

Payment shall be payable at the address of ____________________ (Name of Seller) ______________ located at ______________________________ (Address of Seller). Said payment is due and payable on ______________________ (Date payment due). On non-payment of same, and upon said default thereof, said monies owed shall at the option of the holder and without further notice become immediately due and payable. If, as a result of said default, this note is placed in the hands of an attorney for collection, I hereby agree to pay a reasonable attorney's fee of twenty (20%) percent of the amount due and owing on this defaulted note.

To secure payment of this note, I hereby authorize, irrevocably, the Prothonotary, Clerk of Court or any Attorney of any Court of Record to appear for me in such Court, at any time before or after maturity of said note and confess a judgment against me in favor of any holder of this note with or without filing an Averment of Default, with release of errors, without stay of execution, and for such amount as may appear to be unpaid thereon, together with charges, attorney's fees and costs as herein provided, and I hereby waive and

release all benefit and relief from any and all appraisement, stay or exemption under the laws of any State, now in force or hereafter to be passed.

Witness ______________________ Name of Debtor ______________________

Uniform Commercial Code—FINANCING STATEMENT—For UCC-1

IMPORTANT—Read Instructions on back before filling out form.

The FINANCING STATEMENT is presented to a Filing Officer for filing pursuant to the Uniform Commercial Code. | No. of Additional Sheets Presented | 3. ❑ The Debtor is a transmitting utility.

1. Debtor(s) (Last Name First) and Address(es)	2. Secured Party(ies) and Address(es)	4. For Filing Officer: Date, Time, No. Filing Office

5. This Financing Statement covers the following types (or items) of property:

❑ Products of the Collater are also covered.

6. Assignee(s) of Secured Party and Address(es).

7. ❑ The described crops are growing or to be grown on:*
❑ The described goods are or are to be affixed to:*
❑ The lumber to be cut or minerals or the like (including oil and gas) is on*
*(Describe Real Estate on Item 8.)

8. Describe Real Estate Here: ❑ This statement is to be indexed in the Real Estate Records:

9. Name of a Record Owner

No. & Street	Town or City	County	Section	Block	Lot

10. This statement is filed without the Debtor's signature to perfect a security interest in Collateral (check appropriate box);
❑ which is proceeds of the original Collater described above in which a security interest was perfected, or
❑ acquired after a change of name, identity or corporate structure of the Debtor, or
❑ as to which the filing has lapsed, or
already subject to a security interest in another jurisdiction;
❑ when the Collateral was brought into this State, or ❑ when the Debtor's location was changed to this State.

11. If appropriate in this filing, the terms Debtor(s) and Secured Party(ies) shall respectively mean:
❑ Consignee(s) and Consignor(s), or ❑ Lessee(s) and Lessor(s)

By ______________________
Signature(s) of Debtor(s)

By ______________________
Signature(s) of Secured Party(ies)
(Required only if Item 10 is checked.)

Agreement of Sale of Unborn Foal

An agreement of sale of an unborn foal is simply a contract to sell the offspring of a certain breeding between a specified stallion and a specified mare prior to the actual birth of the foal. This type of contract is often executed well in advance of the actual birth of the said foal, and therefore is considered "executory" in nature. An "executory contract" is a contract that is yet to be executed or performed; that remains to be carried into operation or effect; is incomplete; and depends upon some future performance or event. In this case, the contract can only be enforced at the time when the foal is actually born alive and healthy.

Although these type of agreements are certainly not as common as other types of agreements of sale, they are used for the prepurchase of foals prior to their actual birth and are effective in locking in the purchase of a particular foal upon the terms and conditions set forth in the agreement and at the predetermined mutually agreed upon price by the parties involved.

Agreement of Sale of Unborn Foal

THIS AGREEMENT, is entered into this ______________ day of _________________, 19____, by and between ____________________ ________________________ residing at _______________________ ____ hereafter referred to as "Seller" and ______________________ _______________ residing at _____________________________ __________________________ hereafter referred to as "Buyer".

WHEREAS, Seller is the sole owner of the ______________________ (Breed) mare, ______________________________ (Name of Mare) hereafter referred to as "mare"; and

WHEREAS, mare is in foal to the _________________________ (Breed) stallion, __________________________________ (Name of Stallion); and

WHEREAS, a foal is due to be born on or about the month of __________________________, 19____; and

WHEREAS, both Buyer and Seller are willing to affect an immediate sale of said unborn foal.

NOW, THEREFORE, in consideration of the promises and of the recitals set forth above and the covenants hereinafter mentioned to be kept and performed by Buyer and Seller, Buyer hereby agrees to buy and Seller hereby agrees to sell the unborn foal upon the following terms and conditions:

1. Location of mare and foal.

(a) Seller will, according to the terms of this Agreement, keep and maintain the mare and the unborn foal at _______________________________ (Name of Farm) at no cost to Buyer until such

time as the foal is weaned and possession of the foal is transferred to Buyer;

(b) Seller expressly covenants and agrees that neither Seller nor anyone acting on Seller's behalf shall remove mare or her foal from ________________________________ unless and
(Name of Farm)
until express written consent to the move has been given by Buyer and Seller;

(c) Seller shall give to Buyer thirty (30) days written notice of any such proposed change of location during which time Buyer shall make all appropriate filings or recordings necessary to fully protect Buyer's interest in the foal; provided, however, that in no event shall the mare or foal be located outside of the United States of America or within any jurisdiction within the United States of America which has not adopted the Uniform Commercial Code;

(d) Seller agrees to provide and maintain a suitable environment for the mare and foal with all utilities, housing, appropriate feed, veterinary care and all other reasonable and necessary goods and services for the mare and foal until such time as the foal has been weaned and physical possession of the foal has been given to the Buyer;

(e) Seller shall and hereby does retain full title to the mare; however, so long as the foal is in utero, Seller recognizes Buyer's interest in said foal and agrees not to transfer, lease, sell or in any way hypothecate Seller's interest in said mare. Seller further agrees that until the foal has been weaned, Seller shall not sell or in any way transfer or hypothecate Seller's interest in the mare to any other person unless and until arrangements have been made for the care of the foal which are satisfactory to Buyer. Whether

any proposed arrangements are satisfactory will be at the sole discretion of Buyer, and unless and until Buyer has expressed his satisfaction in writing to Seller no change shall be made;

(f) The term of this Sale Agreement as to the mare and foal shall begin on the date set forth above and shall terminate when all conditions have been fulfilled and physical possession of the foal is given to Buyer.

2. Purchase Price.

Buyer agrees to pay to Seller ______________________________ ($_____________) Dollars as follows:

(a) Upon the signing of these presents, Buyer tenders the amount of ______________________ ($______________) Dollars, the receipt and sufficiency whereof is hereby acknowledged by Seller;

(b) On or before ________________________, Buyer shall deposit in an attorney's trust account the amount which is the balance of the purchase price agreed upon;

(c) The above-referenced balance shall be paid out of the trust account to Seller upon the fulfillment of the following terms and conditions:

(1) Mare foals;

(2) The foal is pronounced live, healthy and insurable by a doctor of veterinary medicine.

(3) Buyer has received written confirmation of full all risk mortality and accident insurance on said foal in the full amount of the purchase price;

(4) Written confirmation by a reputable insurance company, satisfactory to Buyer, has been tendered to Buyer's attorney and said confirmation of insurance shall include the following:

(i) The full amount of insurance shall at least equal the purchase price;

(ii) The beneficiary of the insurance shall be Buyer herein and shall insure his interest in the foal for the full purchase amount; and

(iii) The statement for the premium of said insurance policy shall be sent to Buyer for payment.

3. Conditions Precedent.

Buyer's obligations to deliver the balance of the purchase price shall be subject to the satisfaction of the following conditions precedent.

(a) Mare shall give birth to a live foal by ____________________ (Name of Stallion) ____________________, on or about ____________________, but in no event before ____________, 19_____.

(b) Said foal shall remain alive and in good health for at least ninety-six (96) hours, be sound and be both insurable and in fact insured for the full purchase price against all risks, naming Buyer as beneficiary;

(c) Said foal shall have no white above the knees, but this condition precedent may be waived by Buyer at Buyer's sole discretion (optional clause);

(d) The mare, ______________________________ (Name of Mare) shall be taken to ______________________________ (Name of Farm) and shall remain at said location until the foal is weaned;

(e) A certificate of soundness and good health shall be signed and delivered to Buyer or Buyer's attorney by a doctor of veterinary medicine.

(f) All documents which are required by the ______________ ____________________ (Breed) Horse Registry to effect transfer of the

foal from Seller to Buyer have been executed by Seller and delivered to Buyer or Buyer's attorney. It is understood that should the ______________________________ (Breed) Horse Registry or any other entity or body require any other forms or certificates signed by Seller, Seller shall within five (5) days of receipt, properly complete and execute and return all documents sent to Seller by Buyer;

(g) This Agreement and all other documents to be executed by Seller have been duly authorized, executed and delivered by Seller and constitute valid, legal and binding agreements enforceable in accordance with their terms;

(h) No approval, consent or withholding of objection is required from any governmental authority with respect to the entering into or performance by Seller of this Agreement or the documents to be executed by Seller, or if any such approval is required it has been obtained;

(i) The entering into and performance of this Agreement and the documents to be executed by Seller will not violate any judgment, order, law or regulation applicable to Seller or result in any breach or constitute a default under, or result in the creation of any lien, charge, security interest or other encumbrance upon a foal pursuant to any indenture, mortgage, deed of trust, bank loan or credit arrangement or other instrument to which Seller is a party or by which it or its assets may be bound;

(j) There are no suits or proceedings pending, or to the knowledge of Seller, threatened in any court or before any regulatory commission, board, or other governmental authority against or affecting Seller, which will have a material adverse effect on the ability of Seller to fulfill his obligations

under this Sale Agreement;

(k) The unborn foal has not in any way been sold to or hypothecated to anyone other than Buyer herein; and

(l) There exists no defect or impediment on the registration of the mare, with the ______________________ Horse Registry and the ______________________ Horse Registry will issue a certificate for the foal when born, showing that its sire is ______________________ and its dam is ______________________, and that foal is a duly qualified and registered ______________________ foal.

(Breed) (Breed) (Name of Stallion) (Name of Mare) (Breed)

4. Identification of Buyer.

Seller will, from the date of the signing of these documents, to the date that physical possession of the foal is delivered to the Buyer, clearly identify by appropriate markings and/or in any conversations that the foal is owned by Buyer herein and Seller will expressly advise anyone who inquires or indicates any interest in either mare or the foal that Seller no longer have any interest in the foal and the fact the foal is owned by Buyer.

5. Taxes.

Seller agrees to pay and to indemnify and hold Buyer harmless from all license and registration fees and all taxes, including, without limitation, income, franchise, sales, use, personal property stamp or other taxes, levies and post duties, charges or withholdings of any nature, together with any penalties, fines or interest thereon, imposed against Seller by any federal, state or local government or a taxing authority with respect to the purchase, ownership, delivery, possession, use or transfer with respect to the foal. All amounts payable

by Seller pursuant to this section shall be payable to the extent not theretofore paid on written demand of Buyer.

6. Notice.

Any notice required or permitted to be given by either party hereto shall be deemed to have been given when deposited in the United States certified mail, postage prepaid, and addressed to the other party at the address where indicated on the first page of this Agreement, or addressed to either party at such other address as such party shall hereafter furnish to the other party in writing.

7. Termination by Buyer.

Buyer shall have the right in the event any obligation of Seller has not been met or f ulfilled or if any of the conditions precedent set forth above have not been fulfilled by Seller to terminate this Agreement. Should Buyer do so, Seller shall immediately refund all amounts paid to Seller pursuant to this Agreement. Should Seller fail to do so upon demand from Buyer, Seller agrees to pay all costs and reasonable attorney's fees of Buyer necessary to collect said monies from Seller.

8. Assignment.

Without the prior written consent of the other party, neither party shall assign this Agreement or their interest hereunder.

9. Governing law.

This Agreement shall be construed in accordance with and shall be governed by the laws of the State of ____________________ ____________________________.

10. Default.

In case of default by Seller, it is expressly agreed that Buyer may either revoke this Agreement and demand an immediate refund of all monies paid plus interest at the rate of twelve percent (12%) per annum, or sue for specific performance and demand strict compliance by Seller with the terms of this Agreement, or any combination of the above and/or together with any and all other remedies allowed by law. It is specifically agreed by Seller that should Seller default, whatever remedy or combination of remedies pursued by Buyer, Seller will pay as additional damages all costs, expenses and reasonable attorney's fees incurred by Buyer in enforcing his rights hereunder.

11. Liquidated Damages.

In the event of Seller's default in any of the provisions hereunder, it is agreed by the parties that Buyer's damages could vary widely and would be very difficult to ascertain. Therefore, the Buyer and Seller agree that should Seller default, Buyer has the option of demanding the sum of ____________________ ($_____________) Dollars from Seller as liquidated damages for any of Buyer's claims hereunder. This option shall be of no force and effect unless and until Buyer specifically elects in writing to pursue this remedy. This provision is not provided as a penalty and it is specifically agreed that should this remedy be selected by Buyer and suit be brought to enforce the terms contained herein, that Seller, in addition to __________________ ($__________) Dollars of liquidated damages, will also pay all costs, expenses and reasonable attorney's fees incurred by Buyer in enforcing this provision.

IN WITNESS WHEREOF, the parties have set their hands this ________________ day of ___________, 19____.

______________________________	______________________________
Seller	Buyer
______________________________	______________________________
Address	Address
______________________________	______________________________

Release and Hold Harmless Agreements

Release and Hold Harmless Agreements are essential in today's litigious environment. Any farm or individual which willingly and knowingly allows a third-party to ride a horse owned by the farm or said individual, whether on their premises or not, is today taking substantial risks unless a proper release, waiver and/or hold harmless agreement is properly executed by that third-party prior to that third party getting on that horse. In today's world, that is just a fact of life.

These agreements have become so essential that many insurance companies will not insure any riding establishments unless each and every person who intends to ride at that facility first signs one of these documents.

It is important to note that while these agreements offer some degree of protection, they do not insure that a riding establishment will not be sued. However, these Releases and Hold Harmless Agreements can provide some form of protection and can only be helpful in case of future litigation. It should be pointed out that no agreement will protect a farm or individual from liability unless it is entered into by the other party voluntarily and with full knowledge of the potential risks involved, and will definitely not serve as any legal protection should the farm or individual act in such a negligent or reckless way as to put that other party's life or physical health in danger.

It is advisable that riding establishments establish safety rules and regulations and, thereafter, to enforce them in order to ensure that they are adhered to by all persons. Again, failure to follow established rules created for the safety of the general public may result in litigation and liability whether a person has signed a release and/or hold harmless agreement or not.

The above being said, a riding establishment is far better off having a release and hold harmless agreement being signed by all patrons prior to the patrons getting on a horse than having nothing in writing between the parties. There is, undoubtedly, a substantial benefit in having a writing which can document that a student or patron who gets hurt while riding fully understood the requisite dangers that are inherent with horses prior to his or her getting on or around a horse in question, and had voluntarily assumed the risk of same. These documents definitely offer some form of protection from litigation and potential liability.

In addition, some states are now passing legislation intended to further limit the potential liability of horsemen because of the popularity, but also the recognized inherent risks, of riding horses. One should check with his or her own state legislature to see whether any legislation relating to the above is being actively pursued and enacted in his or her own state.

____
(Name of Stable)

____
(Address)

Release and Hold Harmless Agreement

WHEREAS, the UNDERSIGNED acknowledges the inherent risks involved in riding and working around horses, which risks include bodily injury from using, riding or being in close proximity to horses, among other risks, and further, that both horse and rider can be injured in normal use or in competition and schooling;

IN CONSIDERATION, therefore, for the privilege of riding and/or working, around horses at ______________ (Name of Stable), the undersigned does hereby agree to hold harmless and indemnify ______________ (Name of Stable) and further release them from any liability or responsibility for accident, damage, injury, or illness to the Undersigned or any horse owned by the Undersigned or to any family member or spectator accompanying the Undersigned on the premises of ______________ (Name of Stable).

Date: ______________

____
(Signature)

____
(Print Name and Address)

____

____

____
(Signature of Parent or Guardian)

Release and Hold Harmless Agreement

WHEREAS, the UNDERSIGNED acknowledges the inherent risks involved in riding and working around horses, which risks include bodily injury from using, riding or being in close proximity to horses, among other risks, and further, that both horse and rider can be injured in normal use or in competition and schooling;

IN CONSIDERATION, therefore, for the privilege of taking riding lessons and/or working around horses with ______________________ (Name of Individual) located at ______________________ (Name of Stable), located at ______________________________________, the Undersigned does hereby agree to hold harmless and indemnify ______________________ (Name of Individual) and further release him/her from any liability or responsibility for accident, damage, injury, or illness to the undersigned or any horse owned by the Undersigned or to any family member or spectator accompanying the Undersigned while under the direction and instruction of ______________________ (Name of Individual).

Date: ______________________

____
(Signature)

____
(Print Name and Address)

____

____

____
(Signature of Parent or Guardian)

General Partnership Agreement

Where a partnership is formed among two or more individuals providing for equal rights of management and equal duties for each partner in the partnership, the partnership involved is called a "general partnership". Each partner is liable individually for the debts and obligations of the partnership. It is important to note that this liability may extend past the assets of the partnership to a partner's personal assets. However, despite the fact that each partner is open to this unlimited liability, each partner is also empowered to take meaningful part in the daily management and operation of the business activity. Because this is the simplest type of partnership, a "general" partnership is clearly the most common form of a partnership.

Where a partnership involving two or more individuals is formed which provides for the management to be vested in a general or managing partner, and where the remaining partners are simply investors in the partnership activity, with little or no management duties, the partnership is referred to as a "limited partnership". A "limited" partnership has been more specifically defined as "a partnership consisting of one or more general partners, jointly and severally responsible as ordinary partners, by whom the business is conducted, and one or more special partners, contributing in cash payments a specific sum as capital to the common stock, and who are not liable for the debts of the partnership beyond the fund so contributed." The advantage of a limited partnership, therefore, is that each limited partner's maximum liability is limited to a definite amount, generally his initial investment. The general partner manages the partnership and is personally liable for the debts and obligations of the partnership, if the partnership is unable to satisfy them.

Several years ago, prior to the Tax Reform Act of 1986, many horse partnerships were created in the form of limited partnerships, whereby racehorses or broodmares were purchased with partnership funds contributed by the limited partners, and the major management decisions were made by an experienced managing or general partner. The limited partners' losses were limited to their initial investment and they also received attractive tax benefits with regard to same. As a result of the popularity of these limited partnerships, substantial monies could be raised for investment in horse breeding and racing activities using this vehicle. This especially proved to be a very popular way for new and/or inexperienced individuals to get involved in the horse industry.

However, as stated above, in 1986 the tax law was changed whereby the investor could no longer deduct passive loss investment from any other means of income activity, i.e. annual salary income, if the individual was otherwise not materially actively involved in the day to day operation of the horse partnership business. Consequently, the passive investor in a limited partnership involving racehorses and/ or broodmares could no longer deduct his losses for any particular year until the particular commercial horse activity with which he was involved showed a profit. As a general rule, a horse activity is presumed to be a business and not a hobby activity if it shows a profit two out of every seven years. Since several years over a period of time in a normal horse operation can easily result in losses, the inability of the passive investor to deduct his losses in any particular year from his other ordinary income not related to the horse activity has resulted in the substantial decline of the number of limited partnerships being created in the horse industry. For the record, the commercial real estate market was also affected by this change in the tax laws in a similar way, resulting in a substantial decline in real estate investment in this country.

In addition to the above, and because limited partnerships are considered investment activities, there may be substantial federal and state securities law involvement relating to the creation of a limited partnership. Suffice it to say, that if a horseman seeks to set up a limited partnership, he or she is advised to obtain competent counsel for the creation of the limited partnership to insure that it is done correctly, and to minimize any complications regarding the securities laws and tax laws with regard to same.

It should also be noted that even in the case of a general partnership, there may be serious tax implications. Partnership taxation is a complicated area beyond the scope of this handbook. Any person considering the formation of a partnership to invest in horses should consult with a competent advisor, particularly with respect to the tax requirements.

General Partnership Agreement

______________________________, residing at __________
(name of partner)
______________________________, and __________
(address)
______________________________, residing at __________
(name of partner)
______________________________, hereinafter re-
(address)
ferred to as the "Partners" agree as follows:

1. Type of Business.

The Partners voluntarily associate themselves together as general partners for the purpose of conducting the general business of ______________________________ (type of business), and any other business that may from time to time be agreed on by the Partners.

2. Name of Partnership.

The name of the Partnership shall be ______________________________ (name). This name will be registered in the office of the Secretary of State as the fictitious name of the Partnership.

3. Term of Partnership.

The Partnership shall commence on ______________________________ ("the execution of this Agreement" or specify date). and shall continue until ______________________________ (specify date or "dissolved by mutual agreement of the parties") or terminated as provided in this Agreement.

4. Place of Business.

The principal place of business of the Partnership shall be at ____________________ (address), ____________________ (city), ____________________ (county), ____________________ (state), and any other place

or places that may be mutually agreed on by the parties to this Agreement.

5. Initial Capital.

The initial capital of this Partnership shall be the sum of $____________________, to which each Partner shall contribute by depositing in a checking account in the name of the Partnership at the ________________________ (bank) in ____________________ (city), __________________________ (state) on or before ____________________ (date), the following amounts:

____________________ (name) shall contribute $_______________

____________________ (name) shall contribute $_______________

6. Withdrawal of Capital.

No Partner shall withdraw any portion of the capital of the Partnership without the express written consent of the other Partners.

7. Profits and Losses.

Any net profits or losses that may accrue to the Partnership shall be distributed to or borne by the Partners

____
(in equal proportions or in the following proportions: ____________________ (specify proportions,

____

____.
e.g. _______________ (name), 60 percent; _______________ (name), 40 percent.)

8. Partnership Books.

At all times during the continuation of the Partnership, the Partners shall keep accurate books of account in which all matters relating to the Partnership, including all of its income, expenditures, assets, and liabilities, shall be

(Accrual or Cash)

entered. These books shall be kept on ______________________ basis and shall be open to examination by either Partner at any time.

9. Fiscal Year.

The fiscal year of the Partnership shall end on the ____________ day of ________________ each year.
(Month)

10. Accountings.

A complete accounting of the Partnership affairs as of the close of business on the last day of March, June, September, and December of each year shall be rendered to each Partner within ______________ days after the close of each of those
(Number)
months. On each accounting, the net profits of the Partnership shall be distributed to the Partners as provided in this Agreement to the extent that cash is available for this distribution. Except as to manifest errors discovered within _______________ days after its rendition, each accounting
(Number)
shall be final and conclusive to each Partner.

11. Time Devoted to Partnership.

Each Partner shall devote his or her undivided time and attention and use the utmost of his or her skills and ability in furtherance of the Partnership business.

12. Management and Authority.

Each Partner shall have an equal voice in the management of the Partnership and shall have authority to bind the Partnership in making contracts and incurring obligations in the name and on the credit of the firm. However, no Partner shall incur any obligations in the name or on the credit of the firm exceeding $_____________ without the express written

consent of the other Partner. Any obligation incurred in violation of this provision shall be charged to and collected from the individual Partner incurring the obligation.

13. Salaries.

As compensation for his or her services in and to the Partnership business, each Partner shall be entitled to a salary of $____________ each month, which shall be deducted by the Partnership as an ordinary and necessary business expense before determination of net profits. The salary of any Partner may, however, be increased or reduced at any time by mutual agreement of all the Partners.

14. Net Profits Defined.

The term "net profits" as used in this Agreement shall mean the net profits of the Partnership as determined by generally accepted accounting principles for each accounting period provided for in this Agreement.

15. Withdrawal of Partner.

Any Partner may withdraw from the Partnership at the end of any accounting period by giving the other Partner ________________ (Number) days, written notice of his or her intention to do so.

16. Option to Purchase Terminated Interest.

On dissolution of the Partnership by the withdrawal or other act of a Partner, the remaining Partner, on written notice to the other Partner within ____________________ (Number) days of the dissolution, may continue the Partnership business by purchasing the interest of the other Partner in the assets and good will of the Partnership. The remaining Partner shall have the

option to purchase the interest of the withdrawing Partner by paying to this Partner or the Partner's personal representative the value of the interest determined as provided in Paragraph 17 of this Agreement.

17. Purchase Price of Partnership Interest.

On exercise of the option described in Paragraph 16 above, the remaining Partner shall pay to the person who is legally entitled to it the net book value of the interest as shown on the last regular accounting of the Partnership preceding the dissolution together with the full unwithdrawn portion of the deceased, withdrawing, or terminated Partner's distributive share of any net profits earned by the Partnership between the date of the accounting and the date of dissolution of the Partnership.

18. Buy-Sell Agreement on Death of Partner.

If the Partnership is dissolved by the death of a Partner, the remaining Partner shall have the obligation within ____________________ (Number) days from the death of the deceased Partner to purchase the interest of the deceased Partner in the Partnership and to pay to the personal representative of the deceased Partner the value of that interest as provided in Paragraph 17 of this Agreement. During this ____________________ (Number) -day period following the death of a Partner, the remaining Partner may continue the business of the Partnership but the estate or personal representative of the deceased Partner shall not be liable for any obligations incurred in the Partnership business that are greater than any amount includable in the estate of the deceased Partner that was

previously invested or involved in the Partnership and remained so on the date of death. The estate of the deceased Partner shall be obligated to sell his or her Partnership interest as provided in this Agreement and shall be entitled, at the election of the personal representative of the deceased Partner, either to one-half of the net profits earned by the Partnership business during this ________________ (Number) -day period or to interest for the use during this period of the deceased's interest in the Partnership business at the rate of ____________ percent a year on the value of the partnership interest determined as provided in Paragraph 17 of this Agreement.

19. Duties of Purchasing Partner.

On any purchase and sale pursuant to the provisions of Paragraphs 16, 17, or 18 of this Agreement, the remaining Partner shall assume all obligations and shall hold the withdrawing Partner, the personal representative and estate of a deceased Partner, and the property of any withdrawing or deceased Partner, free and harmless from all liability for these obligations. Furthermore, the remaining Partner, at his or her own expense, shall immediately cause to be prepared, filed, served, and published all notices that may be required by law to protect the withdrawing Partner or the personal representative or estate of a deceased Partner from liability for the future obligations of the partnership business.

20. Dissolution.

On dissolution of the Partnership other than as provided in Paragraphs 16, 17, and 18 of this Agreement, the affairs of the Partnership shall be wound up, the assets of the

Partnership liquidated, the debts paid, and the surplus divided equally among the Partners.

21. Notices.

All notices between the parties provided for or permitted under this Agreement or by law shall be in writing and shall be deemed duly served when personally delivered to a Partner or, instead of personal service, when deposited in the United States mail, as certified, with postage prepaid, and addressed to the Partner at the address of the principal place of business of the Partnership or to another place that may from time to time be specified in a notice given pursuant to this paragraph as the address for service of notice on the Partner.

22. Consents and Agreements.

All consents and agreements provided for or permitted by this Agreement shall be in writing and a signed copy of them shall be filed and kept with the books of the Partnership.

23. Sole Agreement.

This instrument contains the sole agreement of the parties relating to their Partnership and correctly sets forth the rights, duties and obligations of each to the other in connection with is as of its date. Any prior agreements, promises, negotiations, or representations not expressly set forth in this Agreement are of no force or effect.

Executed this _________________ day of ______________________,

19____ at ____________________ County, _______________(State).

____
(Signature of Partner)

____
(Signature of Partner)

Syndication Agreement

Syndication agreements have become more and more popular over the last thirty years, not only with regard to the syndication of stallions, but also with regard to broodmare syndications and racing/showing syndications.

A syndicate is simply a form of group ownership or an association formed for a particular business purpose. The activities of the syndicate will determine whether the syndicate is, in fact, a co-ownership or some other form of ownership. Since each syndication has its own legal characteristics, care should be taken to ensure that the rights of the syndicate members and syndicate manager are clearly and specifically set forth in the written agreement.

Some of the benefits of syndication are the following:

(1) Sharing Risk and Expense. As a result of co-ownership, the risk and expenses inherent to the ownership of a particular horse or horses can be spread among a larger number of individuals.

(2) Diversification. Especially as it relates to racing or broodmare syndications, the ability to include more than one horse in any particular venture allows the syndicate members to spread the risk involved in only owning, racing and/or breeding one horse.

(3) Income and Appreciation. There are significant tax advantages in forming syndications where there is the potential for significant income and earnings.

(4) To Ensure Breeding Rights. Where, as in the case of a stallion syndication, a breeder wishes to ensure his obtaining breeding rights to a particular stallion, the ability to do so may be only through the breeder's actual co-ownership in the stallion.

(5) Stronger Promotion. Especially in the case of stallion syndications, the fact that more breeders may have an ownership interest in the stallion can only help in promoting the stallion by giving that stallion the opportunity to attract better quality mares, which then can, in the future, can increase the exposure of not only the stallion, but also, his offspring.

Stallion syndicates are normally made up of breeders who wish to ensure their ability to breed to a particular stallion. This is a form of co-ownership whereby each syndicate member is responsible for his pro-rata share of all expenses incurred with regard to the ownership of the stallion. These expenses, which include the care, promotion and management of the stallion, are usually expended by the syndicate manager and then reimbursed by the syndicate members. A syndicate member owns the stallion in co-ownership with the other members and receives the right ("nomination") to breed one or more mares to the stallion per year without paying any additional breeding fee. The syndicate member, likewise, can sell his season or breedings to the stallion and does not have to share the proceeds from the said sale with the other syndicate members.

One major difference in the standard stallion syndication agreements concerns the number of breeding rights attached to each ownership interest with regard to any particular breeding season. In the thoroughbred industry, the number of shares normally involved is forty (40) shares, with each share entitled to one free breeding during any particular breeding season. In the standardbred and other breeds where artificial insemination is permitted, frequently more shares are, sold or each share may be allotted more than one breeding.

It should also be pointed out that, like limited partnership agreements, a syndicate agreement may involve a "security" or an "investment contract." As such, investors are afforded protection under Federal and state securities laws to a myriad of investments. Under the Federal and state securities laws, if one sells a security which is not registered or exempt under registration, a purchaser has the right to sue to rescind the sale and obtain a refund, regardless of the promoter's intent or the presence or absence of any fraud. Regulatory authorities can also sue for civil and criminal penalties. Broodmare syndications and racing/showing syndications may fall under the protection of these Federal and state securities laws. Because the basic stallion syndication has been determined by the SEC not to be a security, but a co-ownership by persons who wished to use the property, it is presented here. However, any deviation from this standard stallion syndication agreement should be carefully studied and considered, with the assistance of competent counsel, as to the effect it may have under the securities laws.

There may also be important tax implications. For instance, a stallion syndicate, where breeding rights are sold to the public and the income is returned to all the participants, could be considered a partnership and, therefore, be subject to partnership tax law. It is recommended that any person considering the formation of a syndicate or partnership to invest in horses consult with a competent advisor, particularly with respect to the tax implications and requirements.

Syndication Agreement for

____

(NAME OF STALLION)

AGREEMENT made this __________ day of ____________,
19____, by and between ________________________ residing
at ____; and
___________________________, residing at ______________
______________________________, hereinafter referred to
as "Owners".

W I T N E S S E T H

WHEREAS, Owners are the sole owners of the __________________ (Breed)
stallion, ______________________________ (Name of Stallion), foaled
______________ (Year) by ____________________________ (Sire) out of
______________________________ (Dam); and

WHEREAS, Owners have retired the Stallion to stud service and wish to set forth the rights in and to said Stallion;

NOW, THEREFORE, in consideration of the promises and of the mutual promises of the parties hereto, it is agreed as follows:

1. (a) The ownership of the Stallion shall be divided into ______________ (Number) shares, each share representing an undivided interest ________________ (Percent) in the Stallion. Each of the ______________________ (Number of total shares stated above) shall be on an equal basis with the others.

(b) As of this date said __________________ (Number of total shares) are owned as follows:

(c) The owners of all the fractional interests at any one time shall be known as the "Syndicate members" for purposes of this Agreement.

2. The Stallion shall stand at stud in the name of the ______________________________ (Name of Stallion) Syndicate.

3. ______________________________ (Name) shall be the Stud Manager of the Stallion.

4. The Stud Manager shall manage the Stallion's stud career. He shall have the authority, among other things, to select a veterinarian for, to promote and advertise the Stallion and to determine and set his stud fee and book. The Stud Manager shall act in good faith in the management of the Stallion, but he shall not be liable for such management, including any injury, disease, or death of the Stallion, or of any mare bred, or attempted to be bred to him except for actions or omissions in bad faith or willful misconduct and the Stud Manager shall not be liable for negligence or errors in judgment.

5. The Stud Manager is hereby designated as the Corresponding Officer for the Stallion with respect to the ______________________________ (Breed Registration Authority or Organization; i.e. Jockey Club, United States Trotting Association, etc.) and the Stud Manager is authorized to execute any documents and instruments as he deems necessary or desirable on behalf of the owners to comply with the requirements of the said ______________________________, the various state commissions or agencies, and other governmental or other bodies which he deems to have jurisdiction over the premises herein.

6. The Stallion shall stand at ______________________________ (Name of farm), hereinafter referred to as the "Farm", located at ______________________________ (Address) for his lifetime, under

the sole management and supervision of the Stud Manager, unless the Stud Managers shall elect to move him to another farm affiliated with ______________________________ (Name of farm above). The Stallion can be moved to any farm at any time with the consent of all the owners.

7. The owners shall share equally in the income and expenses of the Stallion in the stud, including but not limited to any property or use tax on the Stallion, in proportion to their respective shares. For administrative convenience, the owners agree that all breeding income is to be paid to and collected by the Stud Manager, and all of the Stallion's expenses incurred shall be paid by said Stud Manager, and they hereby irrevocably appoint said Stud Manager their agent to receive and collect such income and to pay such expenses. The Stud Manager shall prepare and distribute annual reports of the financial affairs relating to the Stallion, and shall distribute the income or bill for net expenses within sixty (60) days of the end of each breeding season. Such annual reports shall show all expenditures and income, the results of the breeding of the Stallion, and such other information as the Stud Manager shall deem pertinent.

8. Each holder of one (1) share in the Stallion shall be entitled to breed __________________ (Number) mare(s) per season to the Stallion without charge for breeding fee. In addition, the following persons shall be entitled to breed the number of mares listed each season free of charge:

______________ (name) ______ (number of mares)

______________ (name) ______ (number of mares)

______________ (name) ______ (number of mares)

These additional breeding rights shall be non-saleable, nonassignable, and non-transferable, except to members of the families of the persons listed above, or the corporations controlled by them, notwithstanding the provisions of paragraph 9 below. The Stallion's normal book shall thus be ______________________ per season, provided, however, that:
(Number of total breedings)

(i) If the Stud Manager with the advice of a veterinarian determines that the Stallion shall be bred to less than the normal book of mares, then each owner shall be entitled to such proportionately fewer breeding rights as the number of breeding rights available bear to ______________________.
(Number of total breedings)
If such a proportionate decrease reduces one or more owner's total rights to less than one, then the Stud Manager shall allocate the breeding rights as he deems fair to all parties, and provided further that

(ii) The intention is that the Stallion shall not be bred to more than his normal book of __________________ mares. If,
(Number)
however, the Stud Manager believes it is in the best interest of the Stallion and the owners to breed to a larger book, then the Stud Manager can set a higher book for one next season. (Note: The total book or mares which can be bred may be limited by the breed registry/organization involved). In such case additional mares may be bred to the Stallion, up to the larger book at the regularly advertised stud fee, and the proceeds received therefrom shall be distributed pro rata to the owners. Such additional breedings shall be offered first to the owners at the regularly advertised stud fee, and if the number of owners requesting the same exceeds the available breeding nominations, the Stud Manager shall determine the owners entitled thereto by lot.

9. An owner may sell, trade or otherwise dispose of breeding rights to which he is entitled for the one next breeding season, at not less than the regularly advertised stud fee, provided written notice thereof is given to the Stud Manager. All mares bred by an owner to the Stallion in any season shall be deemed in use of that owner's free breeding rights to the extent that he is entitled to such rights in that particular season, notwithstanding any sale or attempted sale of such breeding rights.

10. All mares bred to the Stallion by owners must be in sound breeding condition and free from infection and disease, in the opinion of the General Manager of the Farm and/or the Stud Manager.

11. The Stud Manager may procure and maintain public liability insurance in a reasonable amount for the benefit of the owners and the Stud Manager, the cost of same to be borne by the owners.

12. Upon the resignation, incapacity, or death of the Stud Manager, ______________________________ (Name) shall serve as the successor Stud Manager, or if refused, then any individual or entity approved by owners holding at least 75% of the fractional interests in the Stallion.

13. It is not the purpose or intention of this Agreement to create; and this Agreement shall not be considered as creating a joint venture, partnership or other relationship whereby any party shall be held liable for the omission or commission of any other party; but, if for Federal tax purposes this Agreement or the relationship established hereby and the operations hereunder are regarded as partnership, then each

of the parties hereby elects not be treated as a partnership, and further elects to be excluded from the application of all the provisions under the Internal Revenue Code and Tax Reform Act of 1986. The Stud Manager is authorized to execute on behalf of each of the parties hereto such evidence of this election as may be required by Federal Treasury regulations. In making this election each of the parties hereto states that the income derived by him from the operations under this Agreement can be adequately determined without the computation of partnership taxable income.

14. Owners may sell, transfer or assign the share or shares they own hereunder, subject to the right of first refusal in paragraph 15 below, and provided that after any such sale, transfer or assignment, the owner shall remain fully liable to the person or persons who sold such owner his interest for any unpaid portion of the purchase price plus interest, as if no transfer, assignment or encumbrance had been made, unless such selling person or persons agrees otherwise with regard to each and any such sale, transfer, etc.

15. The Stud Manager, on behalf of all the owners, shall have the right of first refusal to purchase any share or shares which an owner may desire to transfer or assign. Any owner who desires to sell, transfer or assign all or any of his shares shall notify the Stud Manager, in writing, stating the amount and terms of his offer (or, in the event the owner shall receive a bona fide offer his notice shall state the name and address of the offeror, the amount of such offer and the terms thereof) and the Stud Manager, as the agent for the other owners, shall have twenty (20) days immediately thereafter in which to accept or

reject said offer on the same terms. The owners shall be notified, in writing, by the Stud Manager, of such offer, and any owner who desires to purchase such share shall notify the Stud Manager, in writing, within ten (10) days after the mailing of the notice. If more than one (1) owner desires to accept the offer, then they shall purchase the offered share(s) in proportion to their present share holdings. If no owner so expresses a desire to accept the offer, then the Stud Manager shall so notify the owner desiring to transfer or assign and thereupon he may consummate the transaction within twenty (20) days after receipt of notice by the Stud Manager to the offeror upon the terms stated in the notice to the Stud Manager. Any transfer or assignment at a date later than the said twenty (20) days shall be subject to the owners, rights of first refusal set forth in this paragraph 15.

16. Upon execution by all parties, this Agreement shall inure to the benefit of and shall be binding upon the parties hereto, their heirs, executors, personal representatives, successors and assigns, and may be executed in several counterparts, which shall constitute the Agreement between the parties as if all signatures were appended to the original instrument. This Agreement shall be governed by and construed according to the laws of the State of ______________.

IN WITNESS WHEREOF, the parties hereto have subscribed their names the day and year first above written.

____
(Name of Owner)

____
(Name of Owner)

____
(Name of Owner)